FITNESS TO WIN

SAIL TO WIN

FITNESS TO WIN

The Complete Guide to Sailing Fitness, Strength & Endurance

Michael Blackburn, BAppSci (Hons), PhD

Exercises demonstrated by Micky Beckett and Matilda Nicholls

FERNHURST
BOOKS

Published in 2026 by Fernhurst Books Limited – Print 1
The Windmill, Mill Lane, Harbury, Leamington Spa, Warwickshire. CV33 9HP, UK
Tel: +44 (0) 1926 337488 | www.fernhurstbooks.com | fernhurst@fernhurstbooks.com

EU GPSR Authorised Representative:
LOGOS EUROPE, 9 rue Nicolas Poussin, 17000, LA ROCHELLE, France
E-mail: Contact@logoseurope.eu

This book is a fully revised and updated version of material which has appeared in previous editions:
First edition (*Sail Fit*) published 1997
Second edition (*Sail Fitter*) published 2001
Third edition (*Sailing Fitness & Training*) published 2010

A catalogue record for this book is available from the British Library
ISBN 9781917801034

Cover photography: Isaac Schotte © Beau Outteridge / Australian Sailing Team

Designed by Daniel Stephen
Printed in India by Thomson Press India Private Limited

MICHAEL BLACKBURN

SPORTS SCIENTIST, OLYMPIC MEDALLIST, WORLD CHAMPION SAILOR & COACH

Michael Blackburn is a world champion sailor, Olympic medallist and coach to multiple gold medallists who has spent his career exploring what drives better sailing, smarter training and performance under pressure.

What sets Michael apart is the rare fusion of elite performance and sports science. Alongside his racing career, he pursued formal research into sailing performance, completing an Honours project on Laser (now ILCA) hiking before earning a PhD examining thought styles and endurance under pressure. His work bridges the gap between academic rigour and real-world racing, translating physiology, psychology and decision-making into faster boats and more resilient sailors.

That blend of experience led to the first edition of this book in 1997. Now in its fourth edition, it reflects over 20 years of elite sailing and 15 years working in applied sports science – refined continuously by athletes, coaches and results at the highest level of the sport. While much of the book's foundation was forged in the ILCA class, the principles are designed to transfer across all sailing – wherever technique, endurance and decision-making determine performance.

As a coach, Michael has been a central figure in one of the most successful runs in Olympic sailing history. He guided Tom Slingsby to three Laser World Championships and Olympic gold at London 2012, followed by Tom Burton's gold at Rio 2016 and Matt Wearn's victory at Tokyo 2020. As Technical Director of the Australian Sailing Team, his leadership helped deliver a fourth consecutive Australian gold medal in the ILCA class at Paris 2024.

Michael continues to work hands-on with coaches and athletes, both on the water and behind the scenes, focusing on the marginal gains that decide races: smarter training, better recovery and clearer decisions under pressure. This book is the distillation of that lifetime of learning – written for sailors who want to understand why things work, and how to apply them when it matters most.

Michael Blackburn sailing a Laser across the Bass Strait (between the Australian mainland and Tasmania) in 2005

Michael Blackburn (left) with his two great rivals in the Laser Class: Robert Scheidt (centre) and Ben Ainslie (right) in 1997. The three went on to stand on the podium together at the 2000 Olympic Games in Sydney: Ben gold, Robert silver and Michael bronze

CONTENTS

Michael Blackburn with Matt Wearn having won the ILCA 7 Olympic gold medal at Tokyo 2020

FOREWORD

I've had the privilege to have Michael as a coach for the good part of a decade where we ultimately finished our coach-athlete relationship with my first gold medal at the 2020 Tokyo Olympics and his third as a coach. Most of this time was in the formative years of my career and the knowledge and experience that Michael had was instrumental in building the foundation of my sailing fitness and has ultimately helped me continue my career with the confidence that I am robust enough to deal with the physical expectations of an Olympic campaign.

Michael doesn't deal in shortcuts or hype. He focuses on what drives progress: consistency, intelligent training and the discipline to show up even when motivation fades. His approach to fitness goes beyond sets and reps; it's about building a body that performs, adapts and lasts.

What I respect is his ability to take complex ideas and make them clear and usable. Whether you're just starting out or you've been training for years, there's something here that will challenge how you think about your own approach.

This isn't a book about chasing extremes or quick transformations. It's about sustainability. It's about doing the work properly, understanding why it matters and developing habits that hold up over time. Michael is honest about that process, the effort it takes, the setbacks along the way and the discipline required to keep moving forward.

If you're expecting gimmicks, you won't find them here. What you will find is a grounded, experience-driven perspective on how to train better, recover smarter and build something that lasts. This has been clearly proven in the sailing world by the legacy that Michael has built and left in the Laser / ILCA class with the Australian Squad since 2008.

I'm proud to introduce Michael's latest work. If you're serious about your training, this book will meet you where you are and push you further.

Matt Wearn
Olympic ILCA 7 Gold Medallist 2020 & 2024
ILCA 7 / Laser World Championships: Gold 2023, 2024; Silver 2018, 2019, 2020; Bronze 2017

MICKY BECKETT & MATILDA NICHOLLS

Micky Beckett and Matilda Nicholls demonstrate most of the exercises in this book. At the time of the photoshoot, Micky was ranked No.1 ILCA 7 sailor in the World Sailing rankings and Matilda was No. 8 ILCA 6 female sailor.

Micky Beckett
Micky represented GBR at the 2024 Paris Olympics in the ILCA 7 class.

Other career highlights include:
Sailing World Championships: Silver 2023
ILCA 7 World Championships: Bronze 2024
ILCA 7 European Championships: Gold 2021, 2025; Silver 2018, 2020, 2022
Trofeo Princess Sofia Regatta, Palma: Gold 2022, 2023, 2024, 2025; Bronze 2026

Matilda Nicholls
Matilda sails an ILCA 6, having moved up from the Laser 4.7.

Her career highlights include:
Laser 4.7 European Championships: Under 16 Gold 2016
Laser Radial World Youth Championships: Silver 2018; Gold 2019
Yachts & Yachting Youth Sailor of the Year, YJA Young Sailor of the Year: 2019
ILCA 6 European Championships: 4th 2022, Silver 2026
ILCA 6 British Championships: Gold 2024
Trofeo Princess Sofia Regatta, Palma: Bronze 2024
ILCA 6 World Championships: 5th 2025

Micky Beckett and Matilda Nicholls

PART 1

INTRODUCTION

From The Author

I entered my first big open-water Laser regatta – the Asian-Pacific Championships – waaay back in 1990. We had five days of 20 to 25 knot winds and triple world champ Glenn Bourke, at his fittest, was loving it, winning five 90-minute races in a row. Back in the fleet I battled it out with others my size (around 70kg – no ILCA 6 back then!) and level of fitness, finishing 41st overall.

My fitness and body weight improved significantly and I went on to finish in the top three in many World or Olympic level regattas including a win at the windiest Laser Worlds I have ever done in South Korea in 2006 at an age when I could have raced in the Laser Masters World Championship.

It took many years of quality training to be fit enough to match it with my biggest rivals at the time – multiple Olympic medallists Ben Ainslie and Robert Scheidt.

This is because the fastest techniques in small boat sailing are tough to do: the trunk is leant well back and thrown forward and / or backwards in response to every wave; the sail is trimmed almost as regularly to keep it at the optimum angle to the wind and every chance to surf the boat down a wave is leapt upon. It requires supreme sailing fitness.

You can get fitter too. Greater sailing fitness comes from:

- Doing training that is specific to the sport
- Progressively increasing the volume (hours) and intensity (how hard) of exercise
- Avoiding injury
- Eating well
- Getting enough rest when you need it

In all but the lightest winds, better fitness – including flexibility, endurance, strength and agility – will make it easier to execute skills like hiking, tacking, gybing and sailing upwind and get you around the course faster. This book doesn't cover sailing tactics and strategy – other books in the *Sail to Win* series cover these areas well. Instead, the focus is on the body and physical factors that can affect performance.

Michael Blackburn winning the 2006 Laser World Championships

Sometime late in high school I did my first dedicated on-the-water training session for sailing (as opposed to weekend club racing), inspired by information from a sports science course. A strong interest in sport saw me study its science for seven years, gaining a PhD, and then putting a lot of that information into practice during a 15-year international career (mostly in a Laser / ILCA 7 plus a season in a 49er along with a few thousand miles of offshore yacht racing).

What's New In This Edition?

Since the first *Sail Fit* book, this project has evolved through *Sail Fitter*, *Sailing Fitness & Training*, and now *Fitness to Win*. Each edition has built on the last, shaped by more experience on the water and in coaching at the highest level – and many thousands of copies have found their way into the hands of sailors around the world.

This fourth edition draws on another 15 years of learning: sailing, training, setting programmes for others and coaching three Olympic champions – Tom Slingsby (2012), Tom Burton (2016) and Matt Wearn (2020). There's more about what works consistently over the long term and what helps you get fitter faster.

It's also the most substantial update yet. The content has been heavily revamped, with clearer explanations, more practical detail and a complete refresh of the design, layout and readability. It's been a pleasure collaborating with Fernhurst Books on this edition; their design and editorial skills have lifted the presentation and overall quality of the book to a new level.

As with all exercise programmes, you should take care when starting and seek medical advice first if you're a real couch potato. A number of exercises in this book are very demanding and should not be attempted without significant background training.

You do not need to be an Olympic aspirant or a gym 'junkie' to benefit from reading *Fitness to Win*. The exercises and ideas in this book are not just for seriously competitive sailors. You may sail mostly in local competitions and go to a bigger regatta once a year to see where you're at; you'll be better than last year if you're fitter and can handle the boat well. The reassurance you get from sailing better will, I hope, help you achieve whatever your goals may be.

Finally, thank you to the reviewers of this edition, especially Jessica Powell, for offering valuable insights.

Good sailing,
Michael Blackburn

This book has evolved over many years to become this latest edition

EXERCISES IN THE BOOK
Different exercises are referred to frequently throughout the book and explained in detail in the appendix. To aid navigation, where an exercise is mentioned which is covered in the appendix, it is shown in ***bold italics*** and the appendix reference in brackets. For example, ***chin up*** (E2). In the appendix it also shows the pages where that exercise is referred to in the book.

Body Weight

Achieving the right body weight for your class eliminates one of the basic excuses in sailing! Suggested body weights for Olympic and small boat classes are given in the tables below. If you are much lighter in body weight than recommended, heavy-weather performance will be predictably poor, however good a sailor you are. If you are much heavier, downwind and lighter wind performance will suffer.

Superior fitness in the muscles used for hiking and sheeting allows a slightly lighter crew to have an advantage on downwind legs, without losing much upwind.

Class	Helm	Crew	Total	Olympic medallists' average (from 2020 or 2024)	Notes
470 Mixed	58-65	71-76	135	135 (63/72)	Assumes female helm / male crew
49er	78-82	80-86	165-168	167 (81/86)	
49erFX	65-70	66-72	135-140	137 (67/70)	
Nacra	75-80	70-75	145-150	150 (78/72)	Assumes male helm / female crew
ILCA 6	68-72			72	
ILCA 7	82-84			84	
iQFOiL Women	65-72			68	iQFOiL sail sizes reduced in 2025
iQFOiL Men	87-95			95	iQFOiL sail sizes reduced in 2025
Kite Women	68-78			74	
Kite Men	85-95			94	

Guideline optimal weight (kg) for sailors of Olympic classes

Class	Helm	Crew	Total
29er	55-60	65-75	120-135
420	50-60	60-70	110-130
505	75-85	80-95	160-180
Aero 5	40-55		
Aero 6	60-75		
Aero 7	70-85		
Aero 9	80-100		
ILCA 4	50-65		
RS200	55-65	60-75	115-145
RS400	75-80	75-85	145-160
Flying Fifteen	75-85	85-95	145-185
Contender	85-95		
Finn	95-100		

Guideline optimal weight (kg) for sailors of international classes

To adjust your body weight to the optimal, you need good exercise and nutrition. For instance, if you're a guy who likes ILCA sailing and want a shot at the Olympics, you may start as a 68kg weakling teenager and struggle for many years to put on weight, but regular training will certainly pay off. It took me three years of serious eating and weight training to grow from around 70kg to around 80kg while adding little fat. For many people it's possible to reach the weight needed for your chosen class but it will take considerable commitment if you naturally fall outside the ideal range.

Check your all-up sailing weight in full kit – boots, jumper, wetsuit, spray top, buoyancy aid (PFD). Step on the scales as soon as you come off the water, wet gear included. Your 'sailing weight' is usually a few kilos above body weight; for example, mine was ~80kg on land but

83-88kg on the water, depending on temperature, wind and how much gear I was wearing. Knowing this lets you tune clothing to the day:

- **Cold, light winds:** Stay warm but minimise water-holding layers – e.g. thin thermal + light neoprene + snug water repellent top
- **Hot, windy conditions:** Prioritise cooling and control – e.g. breathable top, PFD, wetsuit shorts or ¾ suit, sturdier boots – accepting a slightly heavier set-up for better righting moment and comfort

Changing Body Mass

Your body's weight depends on your energy balance. This is the difference between energy in and energy out. Energy in is food and drink (kilojoules). Energy out is in two parts:

- There is the **essential metabolism** which is the energy needed to simply run the functions of the body – digestion, breathing, heartbeat and so on. This can amount to around 50-70 percent of the total. The more muscle and less fat on a body, the faster the basic metabolism
- Then there is **exercise** which consumes energy above the resting level. The energy used here is proportional to the intensity and duration of activity. For active people as much as 50 percent of daily energy expenditure goes on working the muscles and energy supply systems

Gaining Weight

To gain weight, you need to take in more energy than you expend – 'energy in' must exceed 'energy out'. In practice, that means eating more and strength training regularly.

Use resistance training that challenges the major muscle groups – legs, glutes, back, chest and shoulders – with moderate to heavy loads. Aim for 6-12 repetitions per set, performed close to failure with good technique. ('Failure' means you can just complete the final repetition with correct form but could not complete another one.) Compound lifts such as ***squats*** (D3), ***deadlifts*** (D5) and ***presses*** (A15, C2, D2) should form the foundation of your programme. Getting feedback on lifting technique and having a training partner can help you complete heavy sets safely.

A sample weight-training programme and exercise descriptions are given later in the book. Exercises using large muscle groups (thighs and glutes) will add more overall body mass than those using small muscles alone.

If you're under 16, resistance training is still beneficial – but focus on learning proper technique, moderate loads and supervised sessions. Bodyweight and resistance-band exercises (e.g. ***chin-ups*** (E2), ***push-ups*** (C1), shock-cord drills that mimic sheeting) can be excellent for building a foundation.

If you simply eat more without exercising, most of the gain will be in fat stores. When you combine higher food intake with a structured resistance programme, the gain can be mainly lean mass, which is far more beneficial for both health and sailing performance.

Highly active sailors sometimes find it difficult to gain weight. These strategies can help:

- Eat four to five quality meals or snacks a day. Try not to get overly hungry between them. Sometimes you'll need to eat (or drink a shake) even when appetite is low
- Meet macronutrient needs: around 1.6-2.2g protein/kg/day, 4-7g carbs/kg/day, and 20-30% of total calories from healthy fats. Choose whole foods where possible
- Include some lower-fibre, energy-dense carbs (e.g. white rice, pasta, oats, juice) to help meet calorie goals. You'll still get enough fibre if you're eating plenty overall
- Reduce excessive endurance training (long runs or rides) if it limits recovery or appetite. Three heavy gym sessions per week and one or two moderate endurance sessions often work well alongside on-the-water training
- Use liquid calories strategically. Smoothies, milk or blended fruit and protein drinks make it easier to increase total intake
- Add protein and carbs post-session. Aim for 20-40g of high-quality protein (whey or casein) and 0.5-1.0g/kg of carbohydrate within an hour of training to promote muscle growth and recovery. Use third-party tested supplements if you choose shakes

Muscle mass contributes far more to performance than fat, so focus on quality weight gain. If you still need extra buoyancy or warmth, wearing additional clothing layers on the water may be a smarter option than increasing body fat.

When you start training, your energy expenditure rises as your body builds muscle and adapts hormonally. If you're naturally lean, you may even lose a little weight at first – but stay consistent. As your appetite, strength and muscle tissue adapt, your body becomes a more efficient and powerful sailing machine.

Losing Weight

For athletes, reducing body fat comes from maintaining a small, consistent energy deficit while protecting lean mass. When training well, you may even gain some muscle, which can increase basal metabolic rate and help stabilise your target body composition.

Training: Moderate-intensity endurance work – about 30 minutes or more, five times per week – improves your ability to oxidise fat. Cycling, running, swimming and heavy-air sailing are all good choices. To maintain strength and muscle during energy restriction, include two to three gym sessions each week using moderate loads (8-20 reps) with good technique for the main movement patterns. Strength work also supports bone health when training volume is high.

Food focus: Rather than 'cutting fat', prioritise minimally processed foods and let lean protein, quality carbohydrates and healthy fats make up most of your intake. Keep saturated fat modest and include unsaturated sources (e.g. olive oil, nuts, avocado, oily fish). Spreading protein evenly across meals helps preserve lean mass and manage hunger (aim for ~1.6-2.2g/kg/day).

Carbohydrates: Carbs are the body's preferred fuel for training – especially at higher intensities. They're not something to avoid; the right amount supports training quality, recovery and long-term adaptations. Match carbohydrate intake to training load so sessions are well fuelled and the benefits of training aren't compromised.

Rate of loss: A steady reduction of about 0.25-0.5% of body mass per week is ideal for performance athletes, with up to 1% per week acceptable in short phases. Faster losses increase the risk of low energy availability (LEA), fatigue and muscle loss.

Because weight reduction involves a mild energy deficit, some hunger or lower energy levels may occur. Keep the rate modest – alongside adequate protein, fibre, fluids and sleep. This helps maintain training quality and mood. If fatigue, disrupted recovery or irritability persist, increase fuelling and seek professional guidance.

Tracking: Use reliable scales and weigh at a consistent time (e.g. morning after going to the bathroom). Day-to-day fluctuations of 1-2% are normal due to hydration and glycogen changes. Focus on weekly averages and training metrics (mood, power, pace, recovery) rather than single readings and avoid obsessive tracking.

There are no shortcuts to changing body composition – it's a product of sustained, balanced nutrition and consistent training. As you reach your target, continue to prioritise carbohydrates, proteins, fats, vitamins and minerals to stay strong, recover well and perform at your best.

Olympic Gold Medallists in the 470, Malcolm Page (left) and Nathan Wilmot trimmed down for the light winds of Qingdao. Aim to adjust your body weight to suit your chosen class and the likely regatta conditions

Nutrition

Eating well is one of the most reliable ways to boost training quality, recovery and how good you feel doing it. You don't need a perfect diet, just smart habits that consistently support the work you're putting in. With so much generic advice around, this chapter focuses on what matters most for sailors: fuelling before, during and after training and racing in a way that fits real life. Small, steady choices here become a quiet performance edge across the season.

Training Diet

Treat your training diet as a framework, not a set of rules. Fuel for the work required – more carbohydrates on high-load days, moderate amounts on lighter ones – but include some carbohydrate every day. Spread protein across three to five eating occasions, include healthy fats for satiety and energy density, and time fibre and fluids around sessions for gut comfort and consistency. Experiment in training to find what works best for you.

If you feel hungrier during big training weeks, that's normal – eat more of the same quality foods. Aim for four to six eating times per day – a mix of meals and snacks – each with protein, carbohydrate and fluids. Rigid restriction or skipped meals can impair recovery and performance; consistency beats perfection.

Most athletes don't need daily vitamin or mineral supplements. Common exceptions are iron (especially for menstruating athletes), vitamin D (in winter or low-sun exposure) and vitamin B12 for vegans. Check with a sports doctor or dietitian before supplementing.

Useful pairings: Vitamin C-rich foods (e.g. fruit, capsicum) enhance iron absorption from plant foods (e.g. legumes, whole grains). Spinach remains nutritious, but its iron is less bioavailable; combining it with vitamin C sources helps.

Fibre and the gut: Fibre supports health and fullness. If your stomach feels unsettled before training, go lower-fibre for one to three hours pre-session, then return to normal levels afterwards.

	Per 45g serving	Per 100g
Energy	720kJ	1596kJ
Protein	3.9g	8.7g
Fat	1.9g	2.8g
Carbohydrate		
- Total	34.6g	80.1g
- Sugars	7.5g	16.8g
Dietary fibre	3.1g	6.0g
Cholesterol	0mg	0mg
Sodium	98mg	205mg
Potassium	165mg	357mg
Niacin	2.4mg	5.6mg
Vitamin C	10.0mg	22.2mg
Folate	100.0µg	222.2µg
Iron	3.0mg	6.7mg

Nutrition label from a breakfast cereal

- Use the per 100g column to compare foods
- Fibre: Aim for ≥ 3g per 100g
- Saturated fat: ≤ 1.5g per 100g (≤ 3g per 100g acceptable for cheese or yoghurt)
- Sodium: ≤ 120mg per 100g is low; up to 400mg per 100g is fine for most athletes, and slightly higher can help on hot, high-sweat days
- 'Low-fat' isn't always better – a bit of unsaturated fat (olive oil, nuts, seeds, avocado, oily fish) supports energy intake and fullness, especially during heavy training or weight-gain phases

Regatta Diet

Lead Up To Regatta

As competition approaches, training volume typically reduces, but energy needs don't always drop in the same way. Being a little more deliberate with food choices in the days leading into a regatta helps ensure you arrive on the start line well fuelled. The table below provides a simple guide for tuning carbohydrate intake alongside the changing training load in the final days, helping to build energy stores ready for racing.

Days to go	Activity
4	Quality sailing & normal diet
3	Longer sail & extra-high carbohydrates
2	High quality, shorter sail & extra-high carbohydrates
1	Rest
0	Race

Simple pre-regatta activity and nutritional plan

It's important to find a good source of quality food at regattas, whether eating at home or out

Pre-Race Nutrition

Carbohydrate stores: For long or demanding race days, start with full glycogen. If you expect > 90 minutes of solid work, lift carbohydrates to around 8-12g/kg/day for the 36-48 hours before racing while tapering training. For sailing's variable demands, fuel for the work required – eat more carbohydrates when a windy or physically intense day is forecast; keep them moderate on lighter days.

Pre-race meal (1-4 hours before):

- Carbohydrates: 1-4g/kg, low in fibre and fat, moderate in protein
- Include fluids
- Depending on the duration of your race day, it's an idea to have a small top-up 15-60 minutes before the start (e.g. banana, gel or sips of sports drink). Test in training first
- Allow roughly two hours from your last main meal to the race start so digestion doesn't compete for blood flow with working muscles

Caffeine (optional / for windier days):

- 1-3mg/kg for a light boost; up to 3-6mg/kg for stronger effects, taken 30-60 minutes pre-race or split across a long day
- Test in training, monitor total intake, and limit caffeine after 4pm to protect sleep
- Habitual caffeine users may notice smaller effects than others

Stick with familiar foods and fluids on regatta days. The goal isn't perfect eating – it's reliable fuelling that keeps you sharp, steady and ready for the next race.

Once racing begins, the focus shifts from preparation to maintenance – topping up energy and fluids to sustain performance and concentration across races.

Eating On The Water

During prolonged or windy racing, carbohydrate-containing fluids can sustain performance by topping up energy stores and improving concentration. While it's difficult to measure in sailing specifically, research in endurance sports shows clear benefits, so the same principles apply.

Carbohydrate during racing:

- 30-60g carbohydrate per hour from drinks, chews or gels
- Up to 90g per hour on long or very intense days (this higher intake can be trained)

Fluids and sodium:

- Sip regularly, guided by thirst and access on the boat
- Sodium: ~300-600mg per hour (more in hot conditions or for heavy sweaters)

Drink concentration:

- 4-8% carbohydrate (40-80g per litre) provides the best balance between absorption and stomach comfort

Liquid carbohydrates offer dual benefits – energy and hydration. Sports drinks with a 4-8% carbohydrate mix are generally best tolerated. Choose a flavour you enjoy; popular options include Lucozade Sport, Gatorade, Powerade, etc. Drink small amounts regularly – for example, a few mouthfuls on each downwind leg.

Between Races

If you have a short on-the-water break between races, keep food light and easy to digest. Sports drinks (about 500mL over 30 minutes) help top up fluids and carbs without over-filling the stomach. Combine them with small, familiar foods – bananas, low-fat muesli bars or dried fruit – and always test your options in training.

Avoid high-fat or heavy foods such as burgers or chocolate bars; these digest slowly and can leave you feeling sluggish. Wash down solid foods with fluid to aid digestion and re-hydration.

Avoid going too long without fuelling between races, especially on hot or windy days – small, steady intake helps sustain decision-making and reaction time.

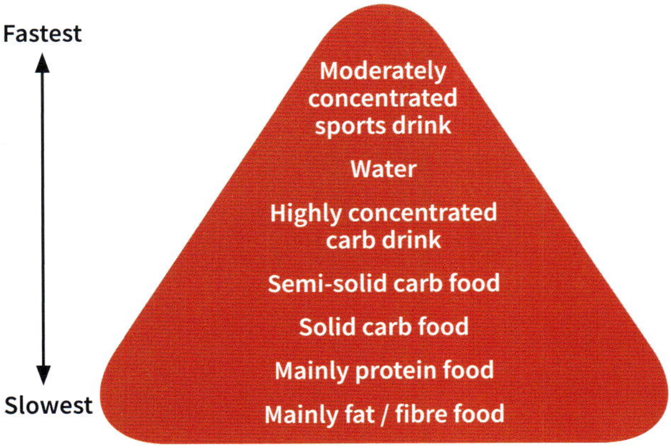

Approximate order of gastric emptying (from fastest to slowest)

So, the message here is to go with the moderately concentrated sports drink during and between races.

Sports drinks are great between races

Post-Race Nutrition

Post-training or post-race recovery is often neglected in the rush to pack up, shower and warm up – often with a well-earned bucket of hot chips! But during a regatta, refuelling soon after racing is essential. Timely recovery nutrition helps restore energy stores, repair muscles and prepare you for the next day.

The recovery window: Your muscles are most receptive to replenishing glycogen in the first two hours after intense exercise. If carbohydrate intake is delayed beyond this, full recovery can take much longer – sometimes more than 24 hours. Aim to start refuelling as soon as practical, ideally within 30-60 minutes of finishing.

Aim to refuel as soon as practical

What to eat and drink:

- Combine carbohydrate and protein in roughly a 3-4 : 1 ratio to speed recovery
- Aim for 1-1.2g carbohydrate/kg and 0.3g protein/kg in this early phase
- Practical examples include:
  - Two to three bananas with a protein shake
  - Low-fat chocolate milk or a smoothie
  - A sandwich with lean meat and fruit juice
  - Sports drinks or recovery formulas (e.g. Lucozade Sport Dual Fuel, SiS REGO, Gatorade Recovery)

Carbohydrate gels (around 50g) or easily digested snacks such as jellybeans, snakes or dried fruit are fine immediately after racing – especially if you can't access a meal straight away. Liquid options help re-hydrate while topping up fuel and are less filling when your appetite is low.

Hydration: Re-hydrate with fluids containing some electrolytes – around 500-1000mL over the first hour after finishing is a good start, adjusting for heat and sweat loss.

Individual response: Everyone's gut tolerance differs, so test your pre- and post-race food choices during training or club racing before major events.

Day-to-day habits: Carbohydrates remain central to the training diet, not just for competition days. Adequate fuelling throughout the week ensures higher quality sessions and better recovery between them.

Good nutrition doesn't mean perfection or restriction. Occasional treats are perfectly fine – what matters is that most of your meals and snacks are built from nutrient-dense, minimally processed foods that support your training and recovery.

Food Preparation

An often-overlooked part of nutrition is what happens to food during preparation. Boiling vegetables such as carrots and peas can cause up to 10-50% of water-soluble vitamins (vitamin C and B-group vitamins such as thiamine and riboflavin) and some minerals to leach into the cooking water. The loss increases with longer cooking times, higher temperatures and smaller cut sizes.

One of the best ways to eat fruit and vegetables is raw or lightly cooked. Steaming or microwaving preserves more nutrients than boiling and using the leftover cooking water in soups or sauces can recover some of what's lost. Frozen vegetables are often as nutritious as fresh because they're snap-frozen soon after harvest, while canned vegetables can be lower in some vitamins but still count as healthy options when drained and rinsed.

Processed Foods

Food processing always involves a trade-off between safety, convenience and shelf life, and sometimes nutrient content. It's not a question of 'processed' versus 'unprocessed' but how a food is processed that determines its nutritional value.

Fuel often (everyday staples)	Fuel occasionally (treats or extras)
Wholegrain or white breads, wraps, cereals	Pastries, pies, sausage rolls
Fruits, vegetables, dried fruit	Chocolate bars, lollies
Low-fat or Greek yoghurt, milk	Hot chips, doughnuts
Lean meat, poultry, fish, eggs	Take-away burgers or pizza
Rice, pasta, noodles, potatoes	High-fat cheese, butter, cream
Nuts, seeds, avocado, olive oil	Sugary soft drinks, energy drinks
Water, milk, electrolyte / sports drinks (during heavy training or racing)	Alcohol or high-caffeine drinks

Smart fuel choices for training and racing

Some foods lose nutrients during processing – for example, potato chips undergo high-temperature frying that increases fat and salt while reducing vitamin C. Others gain nutrients through fortification, such as low-fat or skimmed milk with added vitamin D or calcium, or breakfast cereals enriched with iron and B vitamins.

In practice, minimally processed and fortified foods can fit perfectly within a high-performance diet, while ultra-processed snack foods are best enjoyed occasionally.

Eating Away From Home

Travelling for training or competition makes it harder to eat as you do at home. Planning ahead helps: 'shop from your cupboard' before leaving to pack small, long-life foods such as spreads, oats, rice, pasta, nuts and fruit bars. For overseas trips, consider bringing a small supply of your preferred snacks, recovery foods and sports drinks – especially those that might be difficult to find locally.

When eating out, look for balanced meals with carbohydrates, protein and vegetables. Keep food hygiene, hydration and familiarity in mind – especially before racing – and test any new foods well before competition days.

Sports Drinks

When you're racing in windy or hot conditions, especially for more than an hour, using a carbohydrate- and electrolyte-based drink such as Gatorade or Powerade can help maintain energy and hydration. These drinks combine fluid, carbohydrate and electrolytes – the three things your body needs most during prolonged exertion.

Drinking before, during and after exercise helps maintain blood volume and keeps your heart rate and body temperature in check. Sports drinks were developed to make this process more efficient and convenient.

But which drink is best? Do the electrolytes in one brand make it better than another? Could a simple cordial or fruit juice – often half the price – do the same job? It depends on when you drink it, how long you're active for and how hard you're working.

Carbohydrate Loaders

Carbohydrate-loading drinks are high in carbohydrate – usually more than 10%. Because they're dense, they empty from the stomach slowly and are best used well before or after exercise rather than during. When taken before competition they can help 'top up' muscle energy stores, and afterwards they help replace glycogen used during exercise.

Fluid Replacers

Fluid-replacing drinks are designed for use during exercise. They generally contain 5-8% carbohydrate, a level that provides steady energy while still allowing fast fluid absorption. These are the most common 'sports drinks' on the market and include Gatorade, Powerade and Isostar.

Although brands vary slightly in the type of sugars used – sucrose, fructose, glucose or glucose polymers – their overall energy content is similar.

During exercise lasting more than about an hour, these drinks serve more than just a fuel role. Maintaining a steady carbohydrate intake helps to keep blood sugar stable and reduce the rise in stress hormones that occurs with prolonged hard effort. This not only supports performance but also helps your immune system cope better with the physical stress of racing. Studies show that when athletes consume around 30-60g of carbohydrate per hour – roughly one 500mL bottle of a 6-8% sports drink each hour – the body releases less cortisol and adrenaline, and immune function recovers more quickly afterwards. For very long sessions or events over 2½ hours, intake can be increased to around 90g per hour if tolerated, ideally using a mix of glucose and fructose sources for smoother absorption.

Cooler drinks (around 10-15°C) are absorbed faster than warm ones and can help with cooling in hot conditions. On a racing boat, 'room temperature' drinks are usually the reality, but cooler fluids are ideal whenever possible.

If you're on a budget, cordial or diluted fruit juice can be an acceptable alternative provided it isn't too concentrated. Add a small pinch of salt (only enough to taste) for long, hot sessions to replace sodium lost in sweat.

As a guide, aim to drink about 150mL every 15-20 minutes, or roughly one medium bottle per hour in warm weather.

Nutrient Supplements
Some drinks also include protein, vitamins and minerals. These can be useful after exercise or during heavy training periods to support recovery, but they're not essential for most athletes. Whole foods usually supply similar nutrients at lower cost.

Always check ingredients carefully – under anti-doping regulations you're responsible for any substance found in your body. The Global Drug Reference Online (Global DRO) website is a good place to check whether a product is permitted.

Sports Drinks Summary

Sports Drinks: Types & examples	Energy (kJ / 100mL)	Main uses
Carbohydrate Loaders	**Moderate**	Boosts carbohydrate stores before or after sailing or training
Lucozade	~180-210	
Solid foods (e.g. cereals, rice, pasta)	High (varies)	
Fluid Replacers	**Low - Moderate**	Important during sailing for energy, hydration & to help maintain immune function during long sessions
Cordial / diluted fruit juice	~125	
Gatorade	~120	
Powerade	~130	
Staminade (AUS)	~120	
Isostar	~115	
Homemade (water + juice + pinch of salt)	~120	
Nutrient Supplements	**High**	Adds kilojoule & nutrient intake – good source of protein & carbohydrate for recovery
Sustagen Sport	~1500	
Aussie Bodies Body Bulk	~1550	
Generic recovery shake	1300-1600	

PART 2

SAILING FITNESS

The Fundamentals

Most sailors try to stay active during the week – a run here, a gym session there – so their legs and arms don't let their brains down when it blows 20 knots on the weekend. But if you're honest, how many of those workouts are really designed to help you sail faster?

In a typical windy race, half to two-thirds of your time is spent just trying to keep the boat or board at the right heel angle and the sails working efficiently – hiking, trapezing or pumping. All of it demands strength and endurance through your thighs, hips, core, lower back and arms. The fitter and more conditioned these areas are, the longer you can hold good form – and the less discomfort you'll feel.

The fitter you are, the longer you can hold good form

Running, swimming or general gym work are great for overall health and fitness, but they don't fully prepare your body for what sailing throws at it. The positions and loads are so specific that, without building up the right muscles – or the right endurance in them, you can easily end up sore or even injured once the wind comes on.

Getting fitter won't magically make sailing easy – strong winds will always test you – but it will mean you can push harder for longer, make better decisions under pressure and spend more time near the front of the fleet instead of just hanging on.

Spin classes can be good training for cycling, running is good training for running and swimming prepares you for swimming – but to get truly fit for sailing, we need to sail. There's no better training for the demands of the sport than time on the water.

That said, most of us can't sail often enough to build the fitness we need for racing. So, it makes sense to supplement sailing with exercises that target the same muscles and movement patterns. The key is to choose activities that work the body in a way that's similar to sailing – ones that challenge the legs, core and upper body while demanding both strength and endurance.

Think about it this way: after a spin class or a casual run, do you feel the same kind of fatigue as after a windy day's racing? Probably not. That's because the muscles, loads and positions used in sailing are unique. Hiking, trapezing, sheeting, foiling and pumping all involve long periods of static or repeated effort in awkward positions that most gym or cardio classes simply don't mimic.

Only exercises that closely match these demands will directly improve your sailing fitness. It's a bit like expecting world-class hockey players to spend most of their off-field training time swimming laps – it's great for general conditioning, but not for the specific movements and muscle use they rely on.

The relative value of different exercises for sailing is illustrated in the graph: the higher the rating, the more specific and beneficial the activity is. The exercises are scored according to how closely they match sailing – in terms of muscle use (legs, core, shoulders and arms), type of contraction (often static or sustained) and the continuity of effort (almost non-stop in hiking, sheeting and pumping). Choosing activities higher on the list will give you the biggest return for your time and effort.

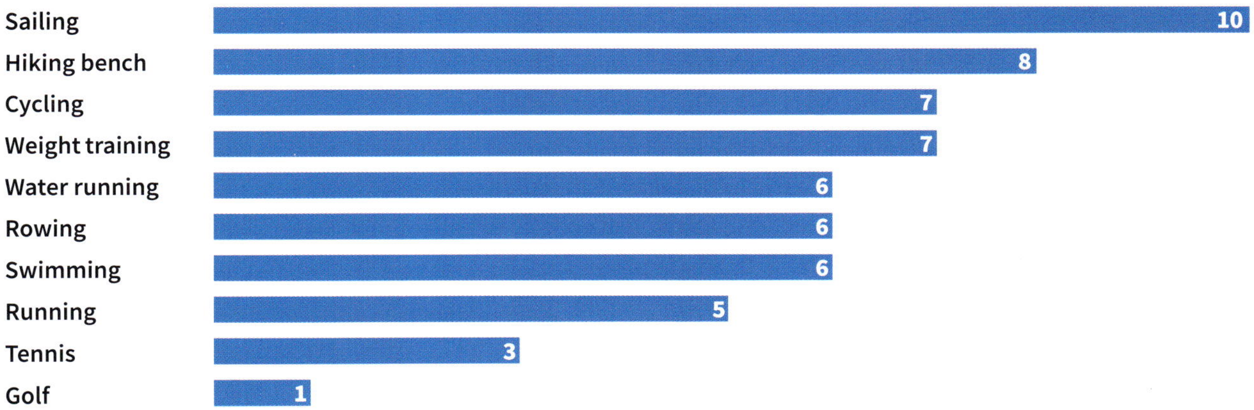

The value in sport-specific training: Ratings out of 10 for different sports and exercises to physically train for small boat sailing

Cycling, hiking benches, water running (waist-deep) and weight training all give the thighs a solid workout, and with consistent effort will help improve the endurance of the muscles used for hiking. Focus on these activities to hike longer and stronger during a race.

Across a week, aim for roughly 35 points worth of sailing-related activity, using the numbers in the graph. For example:

	Points
One windy weekend race	10
One 45-minute bike ride	7
Two weight training sessions (40-45 minutes)	14
30 minutes on a hiking bench	8
	39

The more specific the activity, the more efficient your training will be. Full-time small boat sailors typically reach 70-100 points a week.

Occasionally including a lower-ranked activity isn't a bad thing. Different types of exercise place new stresses and strains on the body, which can help prevent overuse injuries and add variety to your training week.

Swimming is also valuable because injuries are rare and it gives a whole-body workout. Its value for sailing can be increased by using flippers and doing kick-only laps. Use stiff, medium-length fins to exaggerate the work done by the thighs, hips, buttocks and ankles – the same muscles that matter when hiking.

Training (Variables & Principles)

Training Variables

Training variables are the levers you adjust in any programme – namely intensity, duration, frequency and volume.

1. **Intensity:** Heart rate is a good, simple and accurate indicator of exercise intensity. Roughly, you will need to work in a heart rate range of 120-160 beats per minute to make gains in aerobic fitness. To increase your strength, say, to lift your boat, your muscles will need to do repeated short, hard efforts, with a suitable rest afterwards
2. **Duration:** You need to work over a long enough period (30+ minutes) to improve your aerobic fitness and strength. Typically, an aerobic workout would be more continuous in activity than a session designed to improve power or strength. A really long session (2-4 hours) is OK if you are fit enough to handle it, but it may mean you will need more rest before the next session
3. **Frequency:** Three training sessions per week is usually regarded as the minimum number to make steady gains in aerobic fitness or your muscle's strength. However, top Olympic sailors usually do 8-12 different sessions per week
4. **Volume:** When you multiply frequency by duration you get volume. It's usually measured per week. Minimum volume would be about two hours per week. Maximum volume depends on your fitness, but let's say that 20-25 hours a week is a lot!

Principles Of Training

Before getting into specific exercises, it helps to understand the basic rules that make training work. These simple principles apply to every successful fitness programme – whether you're preparing for a world championship, weekend racing or just wanting to feel stronger and last longer on the water.

Every good training programme, for sailing or any other sport, is built on a few key principles. Understanding these helps you train smarter, improve faster and avoid injury.

1. **Overload and progression:** To get fitter, you have to ask your body to do a bit more than it's used to. That might mean a longer session, higher intensity or shorter rest. As your body adapts, you gradually increase the challenge to keep improving
2. **Specificity:** You'll get the biggest return from training that looks and feels like sailing. The closer your exercises match the movements, muscles and energy demands of your class, the more useful they'll be on the water
3. **Recovery, rest and adaptation:** Training makes you tired; recovery makes you stronger. Improvement happens when the body repairs and adapts after the workload, not during it. Build in time for rest, easy days and proper sleep – they're all part of the programme
4. **Reversibility:** Fitness doesn't hang around forever. If you stop training, you'll gradually lose the gains you've made – the old 'use it or lose it' rule still applies
5. **Individuality:** No two sailors are the same. Age, body type, training history and even personality all affect how you respond to training. What works for your teammate might not be right for you
6. **Variation and periodisation:** Doing the same thing every week eventually stops working. Mixing up the intensity, duration and focus keeps you improving and helps prevent injury or burnout
7. **Maintenance:** Once you've built a solid base, you don't need to keep pushing harder all the time. A smart, consistent programme can maintain your fitness with less effort between key regattas

Building sailing fitness isn't about spending endless hours in the gym – it's about training with purpose. Focus on quality over quantity, choose exercises that reflect the demands of your class and use the principles of training to guide how hard, how long and how often you work. The better you align your training with what actually happens on the water, the greater your progress will be once you're back in the boat.

Next, we'll look at how to train specifically for hiking – the most demanding and distinctive movement in small boat sailing, and the one that most often decides who goes fastest upwind.

Focus on quality over quantity, focusing on the demand of your class

Hiking: No Walk In The Park

At least since the 1950s, small boat sailors, including the legendary Paul Elvstrom, had cloth straps along the centreline of their boats. The feet were hooked under these straps, so that the whole trunk could be held beyond the edge of the boat. This addition dramatically improved the speed of sailing dinghies in strong winds because a far greater righting moment could be exerted by the body to balance the wind's heeling force. This leaning out over the side of the boat is known as hiking – the most dreaded activity in small boat sailing!

There is a definite limit to how long small boat sailors can hold an effective hiking position. Felt your legs start to burn even before the end of the first beat? Hiking involves static contractions of the large muscles of the thighs and trunk. Static contractions involve a muscle developing tension without making the joints move. These contractions are dominant in small boat sailing – other examples are holding the mainsheet and gripping a windsurfer boom.

Even at relatively low levels of static muscle tension, the blood vessels are squeezed heavily and the ensuing reduced blood flow and oxygen to the muscles will rapidly cause pain and fatigue. This discomfort must be tolerated in training to develop the muscles so they can better handle the demands of competition sailing.

In addition to the continual muscle strain of hiking, there is also the need to carry out active movements of the arms and trunk to trim or pump the sail(s), steer and physically drive the boat through waves. The intensity and nature of the physical activity during sailing, and the optimal physical characteristics of the sailors themselves, obviously depend on the class of boat sailed.

Foiling boats (Moth, Waszp, Switch) can demand more arm work while hiking – constant, active sheeting to track rapid apparent wind changes. The hiking geometry also shifts with windward heel and greater freeboard, allowing a slightly more bent-knee posture while keeping the trunk projected out; this lengthens the quads and can improve endurance. As in the ILCA, when conditions turn technical (gusts, confused chop), back off the hike intensity a fraction to focus on accurate steering and active sheeting.

The key hiking, sheeting, pumping and trapezing muscles are shown in the photo below and the actions they perform summarised in the table overleaf.

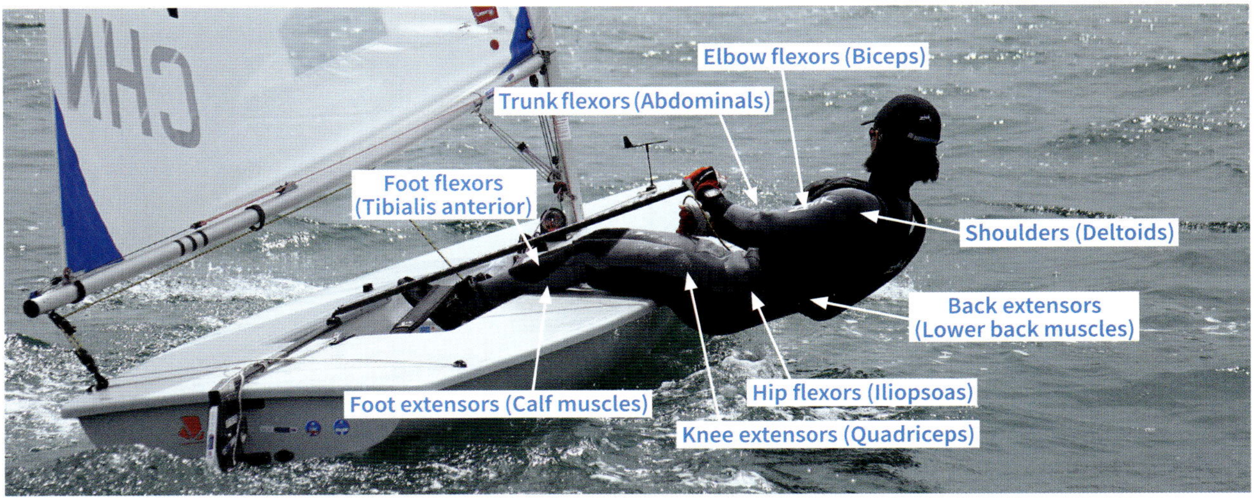

While all forms of sailing will use many of the body's muscles, usually a few key muscles fatigue first – and these need special attention in training

Main muscles	Actions
Knee extensors (Quadriceps)	Hold the legs straight while hiking or standing
Hip flexors (Iliopsoas)	Hold the trunk up while hiking by joining the thighbone, hip & lower back
Foot flexors (Tibialis anterior)	Lift the toes up while hiking – helps with balance when standing
Shoulders (Deltoids)	Pull the arms backwards during sheeting & pumping
Elbow flexors (Biceps)	Bend the arms during sheeting & pumping
Trunk flexors (Abdominals)	Stabilise the spine by linking the ribs & pelvis – the 'core'
Back extensors (Lower back muscles)	Support the lower back during the range of trunk movements
Foot extensors (Calf muscles)	Point your toes while trapezing or sailboarding & thereby help with balance

The key hiking, sheeting, pumping and trapezing muscles and actions

Research On Hiking

Scientific studies have examined the physical demands of small boat sailing and the toll it takes on the body. For my own study, I focused on the ILCA class, as these sailors rely heavily on hiking endurance to perform well, and there had been little previous research in this area.

To create a realistic test, I first analysed video of skilled ILCA sailors racing in windy (12+ knots) national-level events to profile typical race activity – including leg lengths and tacking frequency. Based on this analysis, a dinghy sailing ergometer was designed and built to simulate a full race with upwind, downwind and reaching legs, as well as tacking. This dry-land device replicates the physical demands of small boat sailing without going on the water.

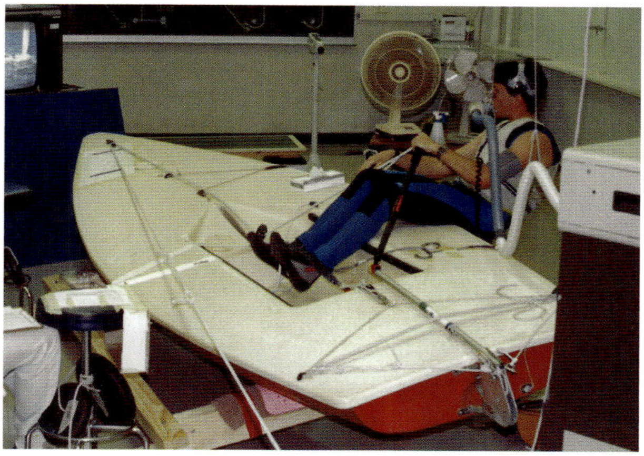

A full ILCA hull is used in this hiking test. Mainsheet and tiller are loaded while the sailor's righting moment over a set period is recorded.

During testing, sailors watched race footage of an ILCA sailor following the protocol while hiking on the ergometer in the lab, matching the on-the-water movements in real time. This set-up allowed detailed measurement of what happens in the body during sailing and helped identify what separates those who can hike harder and longer from those who cannot.

Key Findings

Simulated dinghy sailing raised the subjects' blood pressure sharply and involved a modest and steady rate of energy use by the body. The use of aerobic energy during the three 20-minute upwind legs was 40 to 60 percent of the subjects' maximum – indicating only a moderate level of exertion. However, during the upwind legs, blood pressure was extremely high. In fact, blood pressure levels matched those you'd normally find during really heavy cycling – indicating how strongly the muscles contract when hiking to restrict blood flow. As you may expect, both blood pressure and aerobic energy usage were significantly lower during the downwind legs.

Other results indicated that the combination of body mass in sailing clothing, thigh muscle strength, hiking strap length, aerobic fitness and the blood pressure response to hiking all contributed to the sailors' hiking performance. In short, body size, strength and aerobic fitness are all related to how effectively you hike, so it is worth working on each of these factors.

A separate study determined that around 25 percent of the thigh muscle's strength is used when hiking. Static contractions of the thigh muscles at this level will fatigue the muscle very quickly – within five minutes. But the discontinuous nature of hiking – with periodic rest periods thrown in (tacking, going over waves) – allows small boat sailors to sustain the static contractions for much longer than five minutes. In practice, this means that if there is no detrimental effect on the trim of the boat and sail, the body movements you make while hiking can and should be exploited to improve your endurance.

Something that can make those movements easier is a comfortable, wide hiking strap. Hiking straps vary in the width of padding, the covering material and the thickness and quality of the padding itself. A covered strap with dense foam padding that will not fold over on itself is probably best so that the instep of the foot is not rubbed raw. Standard width is the seat-belt style 50mm, however, I used to source a 70mm wide webbing for my hiking straps, so the feet had more surface area to contact when hiking. Wider straps can be purchased from manufacturers such as Zhik.

What Science Tells Us About Hiking Performance

Research into the physical demands of hiking has given us a clearer picture of what really limits performance – and what helps improve it. By combining findings from my own studies with more recent research, we know that hiking ability depends on several key factors:

- Body mass (including clothing)
- Height
- The strength and endurance of the quadriceps, core muscles and hip flexors

The following points translate this science into practical ways to improve your hiking technique, endurance and comfort on the water.

Technique & Position

- **Hiking strap set-up:** Setting the hiking strap longer – or hiking off the toes – allows you to hold your body further out for greater leverage and righting moment. The trade-off is higher muscle load and reduced endurance. Many sailors use adjustable straps to suit conditions – typically tighter in light winds and on reaches, and looser upwind in stronger winds. Others

Hiking: The thigh muscles are usually felt to fatigue first, but there are a number of other important muscles – more on this ahead

prefer a fixed strap to eliminate another variable during racing

- **Varying hiking positions:** Use a flat-out, high-effort position for starts and tactical moments, then shift to a more efficient, sustainable posture once you've established control (for example, the second beat with a lead). As your leg endurance improves, you'll hold stronger positions longer – it won't necessarily feel easier, but your average speed will increase
- **Micro-rests and pacing:** You can extend hiking endurance by taking brief 'micro-rests' to restore blood flow – for example, easing muscle tension as you crest a wave, or subtly swapping your weight between your legs. Recognise early signs of fatigue and time these short relaxations before exhaustion builds. Even the few seconds out of the straps during a tack can make a difference
- **Leverage:** The further out you can hike – even if only your toes are under the strap – the faster you'll go. The stop-start rhythm of real hiking explains why leaning from a hiking bench in a static position feels harder, but it's still one of the best ways to build sailing-specific strength and endurance

Conditioning & Training

- **Hiking bench practice:** Make your hiking bench work realistic by copying your on-the-water movements. Watching a video of yourself or a top sailor and matching the actions helps train the same coordination and timing you use in the boat
- **Aerobic conditioning:** Hiking endurance isn't just about leg strength – aerobic fitness plays a key role. A well-conditioned heart and circulatory system handle the high blood pressures and oxygen demands of hiking more effectively. Cycling is particularly good because it uses the same thigh and hip muscles. Rowing machines are also useful for combining leg and upper-body work, helping with both hiking and sheeting strength
- **Strength training:** Building leg strength through weight exercises such as ***squats*** (D3), ***leg presses*** (D2) and ***extensions*** (D1) improves your ability to hike from the strap and reduces the temptation to support yourself with the mainsheet, the stay or your sailing partner

Hiking Pants & Padding

- **Padding and comfort:** Proper hiking gear can dramatically reduce pain and extend endurance. The backs of your thighs should be well padded to spread pressure from the gunwale and maintain blood flow. A single thin wetsuit layer is rarely enough at performance level – adequate padding significantly reduces pain and helps you stay powerful through long upwinds
- **Options and fit:** Good choices include full-length battened hikers such as the Rooster Pro Hikers or Zhik Hiker Suit. Fixed-batten hikers provide consistent support and a solid platform, while removable systems like Zhik PowerPads let you adjust pad position and stiffness or move them between suits. Choose the system you'll actually wear for long sessions because comfort, fit and pad placement matter far more than brand
- **Care and maintenance:** Always rinse your hikers or wetsuit in fresh water after sailing. Dry them in the shade – inside out first, then right side out – and avoid heat sources such as car boots, hot water or tumble dryers
- **Key takeaway:** Well-fitted hiking pants or pad systems with correctly placed battens are essential kit. They may cost more, but they dramatically reduce pain and extend sustainable hiking time – translating directly into faster average speeds and better results

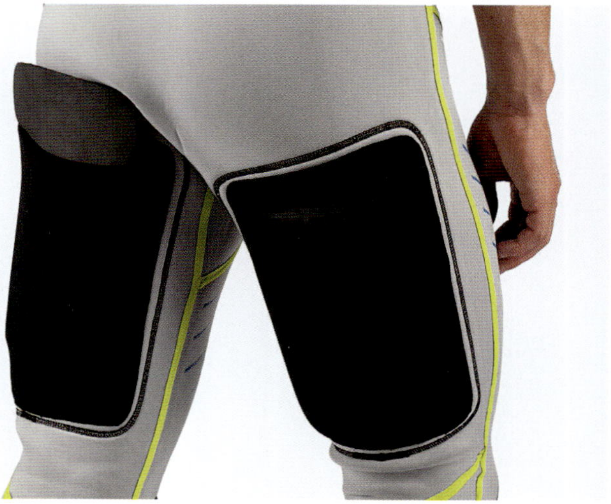

Internal view of Zhik hikers

Footwear

- **Purpose and design:** Good footwear makes a big difference to comfort and control. Hiking boots protect the instep, provide grip and support the ankle, all while reducing pressure points
- **Support and fit:** Lace-up boots generally offer better ankle stability than zip-up or stretch neoprene types. The Zhik Hiking Boot is a strong example, though any supportive boot with firm padding will help
- **Light wind sailing:** In lighter winds, heavy rubber boots can make movement clumsy, so many sailors prefer bare feet for better feel. Choose the set-up that gives you the best mix of grip, flexibility and protection for your boat and sailing conditions

Good hiking boots and a padded hiking strap can make hiking more comfortable

Understanding the science behind hiking performance is the first step. Next, we'll look at how to apply that knowledge through advanced hiking technique – refining posture, timing and movement to turn strength and endurance into on-the-water speed.

Advanced Hiking Technique

I originally thought that the best small boat hiking position involved a bent body, that is, a fair degree of bend at the knee and hip joints with the bottom just skimming the waves. I figured hiking like this would be unbeatable over a long race because the muscles work more efficiently in this position compared to hiking with the legs straight and trunk laid well back. High tension in the muscles when hiking flat-out restricts blood flow and limits the energy available in the muscle, making you tired more quickly. The bent body position is quite difficult to hold properly anyway, so I thought that setting a fitness-training goal of being able to hold this position for a full race would be reasonable. However, I was wrong – there are ways to hike harder.

Years ago, a couple of top Laser sailors pushed hiking posture further and quickly found extra upwind speed. They tightened their straps and hiked off their toes, which effectively locked the ankles and forced straight legs. With the fitness to hold the trunk almost flat, they could hike a little harder and more consistently than everyone else.

Replicating this takes years. The position puts large loads on the ankles and hips, which aren't designed for prolonged work in that range. You need time to condition the tendons and ligaments of the ankles, knees and hips – and to build a strong core to link the legs to the upper body – so the body can tolerate the strain.

These sailors reasoned that maintaining a high righting moment while sailing the boat flatter would make them faster upwind in a breeze. By tightening the hiking strap and lengthening the tiller they could hike off the tips of their toes with their legs and body extended and held well above the waves and hold both the mainsheet and tiller hands near chest level.

Hiking off the toes and leaning back further is harder but faster

Basically, the aim of the technique is to lock into the boat and provide lots of leverage. You need to keep your head almost level with your knees and eyes looking down the end of the tiller extension. It is a funny feeling at first because your head is at a different angle and you can't see as much. And it is physically quite hard. However, you can focus on sailing the boat flatter and on gaining extra speed and height.

To lay your body flatter while hiking, you need good flexibility of the hip muscles and strong core-stabilising muscles – these support the trunk while hiking. The hip muscles need to be long enough so that, when the trunk is lent back, they're not at the limit of their range of motion. The stronger the core, the better it can support and stabilise the spine against the pull of the hip and other muscles. Therefore, the hip muscles should be stretched especially well before and after sailing, and the core needs consistent training to help keep the spine in good shape when hiking flat out.

It is interesting to compare how hiking positions have changed with the advent of battens in hiking pants and the 'far-out on-the-toes technique' (see diagrams). The thighs of a sailor wearing only a wetsuit or shorts squash over the gunwale. This restricts blood flow and lowers the body to the oncoming waves. Hiking pants with battens lift your bottom higher off the water and prevent the gunwale stabbing into the back of the thighs.

To lift yourself even higher, tighten the hiking strap so the feet are held down lower, and slide thicker battens into the hiking pants. Also, to maximise righting moment, lean back further and hold the hands up high, steering and trimming the sheet from chest level. Of course, the only trouble is that the position is much harder to hold! But it's ideal for blasting off the start line.

A tighter hiking strap actually gives you a good variety of hiking positions. In light to moderate winds where you don't need to hike so hard you can sit in slightly and hike off the instep of your feet. Since you're locked in tightly to the hull in this position it makes it easier to 'torque' the boat – that is, steer it by throwing your body forward or back. On the reaches the tighter strap makes it easier to keep your backside out of the waves. Then when it really blows, simply slide out to your toes – there's no need to adjust the length of the strap and you have a variety of hiking positions.

A repeated warning: **Hiking off the toes must be approached gradually to strengthen the ankles.** The best approach is to tighten the strap gradually over a period of months and slowly spend more time swinging from your toes.

Note that your height and the design of the boat will determine whether hiking off the toes or the instep of the feet is best. If you are taller than 188cm (6 foot 2 inches) or so you probably will be able to get out far enough by hiking off the instep. Shorter, like me, and hiking from lower down the foot seems to feel more powerful with a tighter strap.

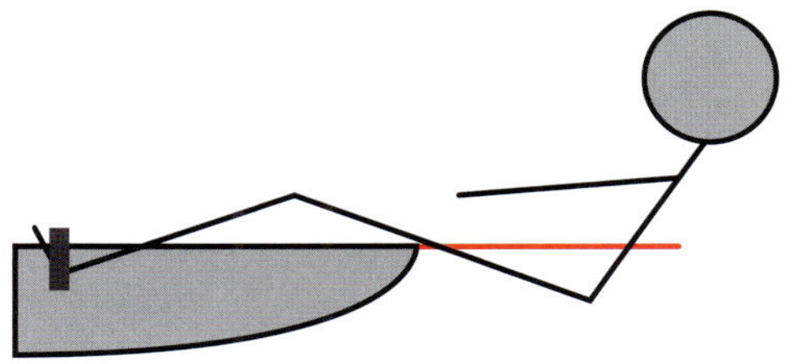

Wetsuit only

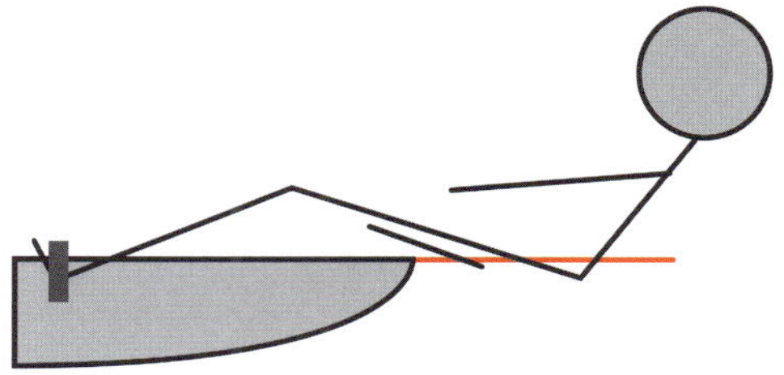

Hiking pants with battens

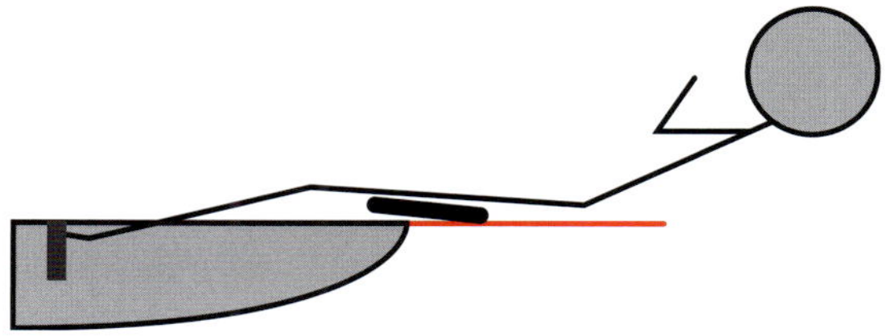

Hiking pants, thicker battens, hiking off toes, tight strap, arms high and relaxed, leaning further back. With battened hiking pants and more aggressive hiking, the top sailors hike with their bodies further out and bottoms riding higher above the waves to sail faster and point higher. Think about hiking 'up and out'

Note that on some dinghies, the hiking strap is so close to the gunwale that your knees are naturally within a few centimetres of the gunwale. In this case, you will have little choice but to hike off the instep of your feet.

Never sacrifice accurate sail trim and steering for raw hiking effort. I recommend sailors aim for ~90% hike at the most so they can keep sail trim, heeling and steering precise. If you over-hike, you may generate more righting moment, but you'll sail less accurately and fatigue sooner.

Trapezing

At the start of the last chapter, I mentioned that toe or hiking straps had been around since at least the 1950s. Interestingly the trapeze dates from even earlier with the likes of Beecher Moore, Austin Farrar and Peter Scott experimenting in the 1930s. These early systems were crude by modern standards and were often restricted or banned under class rules at the time. Trapezes are now common across many classes, with clear implications for how sailors train and prepare physically.

Trapezing Fitness

Trapezing shifts the athletic emphasis up the chain: trunk, scapular stabilisers, shoulders and forearms do much of the work that ultimately controls boatspeed. The job is often periods of stillness on the wire punctuated by sharp, high-intensity bursts for tacks, gybes and spinnaker work. That pattern demands isometric endurance – especially through the core, glutes, calves and grip – plus the ability to spike power and coordination on demand without losing trim or balance.

Dry land conditioning should mirror the sport's intermittent nature. Use blocks of steady work at moderate effort – like a sustained upwind hold – punctuated by short, harder efforts that simulate two or three manoeuvres in a row, then a settle. Circuit formats, rower or air-bike intervals or on-the-water drills that cluster manoeuvres work well.

The aim of strength training for trapezing is to build robustness rather than chase one-rep numbers. Key target areas include:

- Core stability
- Horizontal and vertical pulling for shoulder strength and balance
- Trunk anti-motions (anti-extension and anti-rotation) to maintain a tall, steady posture on the wire
- Calf / ankle strength to hold narrow foot placements and connect to the boat with confidence

Off the water, keep exercise selection simple and progress by adding small amounts of time under tension. For example, run a 12-15-minute continuous circuit with simple gear:

- 45-second ***chin-ups*** (E2) (assisted as needed) or ***body-weight pull-ups*** (E5) under a sturdy table / rings

Trapezing requires its own kind of fitness

- 30-second ***split-squat hold*** (D3) (switch legs half-way through each round)
- 30-second ***towel dead hang*** (E4)
- 40-second ***Copenhagen plank*** (H5) (switch sides halfway through)
- 60-second skipping at easy pace to 'settle'

Repeat for 3-4 rounds.

Balance and agility deserve deliberate practice. Getting on and off the wire demands reactive footwork, accurate foot placement and the ability to decelerate, turn and re-accelerate with the boat moving beneath you. Short change-of-direction drills, ***lateral bounds with controlled landings*** (D8) and ***single-leg balances*** (D9) translate directly to more accurate, agile and faster crossings.

Shoulder care is really important. In the gym prioritise scapular control – think 'shoulder blades first'. On ***pull-ups*** (E5), start by setting the blades down and slightly back (neck long, no shrug), then finish each rep by gently squeezing the blades together and return them smoothly before the next rep. Keep your pulling volume higher than pushing (e.g. more ***bench rows*** (E6) than ***bench press*** (C2)). Vary grips and handle diameters to spread load and avoid overuse at the inner elbow and wrist. Pulls can be done with a bar, a thick rope or even a towel for variety.

A highly effective, low-cost addition is land-boat training. Tie the boat down on a flat surface, rig a boom and set basic controls so sheet loads feel realistic. Rehearse the full trapeze sequence – clip-in, extend fully, mimic some trim changes, move in, unhook, cross, re-hook. Build to clustered reps (two or three rapid tacks, or a tack-gybe-tack), then a short settle while holding the position on trapeze. This grooving of foot placements, boom clearance, harness timing and sheet hand-offs happens without weather, traffic or risk. It's also the safest way to coach position relative to the gunwale and hand transitions under light fatigue. Use a timer to set and keep track of the intervals and film a few sets to check movements, posture and hand habits. Even 15-20 minutes a couple of times per week pays off quickly on the water.

Because blood flow is restricted during long holds, integrate small 'micro-moves' on the wire – subtle ankle pumps, gentle posterior-tilt-to-neutral of the pelvis, brief scapular resets – to restore perfusion while maintaining a steady platform. These are tiny corrections rather than fidgets; done well, they preserve feel, delay forearm fatigue and help you keep projecting without stiffness setting in. The aim is good posture, relative relaxation and maximum projection from the boat; if one element slips, adjust minimally and return attention to boatspeed.

After sailing, two or three focused mobility drills will help maintain your usable range of motion:

- For hip flexors, use a couch stretch or half-kneeling lunge with a posterior pelvic tilt (glute on), holding for 30 seconds per side
- For thoracic extension, lie over a foam roller at mid-back and gently extend for 6-8 slow breaths in 2-3 spots, then add 'open book' rotations for 6-8 reps per side
- For ankles, move slowly through both directions (point the toes, then lift them up), then finish with straight- and bent-knee calf stretches for 20-30 seconds each

Keep positions pain-free, breathe quietly and stop short of any pinchy joint sensation.

Practising drills on land

Finally, bake in a little monitoring. Track a simple set of readiness markers – subjective grip endurance, ability to hold a stable posture on the wire for a timed upwind, ***towel dead-hang*** (E4) time, ***single-leg calf hold*** (D10) – so you can nudge training up or down before overload becomes injury.

Trapezing is about being unshakeably steady when nothing is steady; build the capacity to hold a robust posture, then layer on the agility, grip and timing to move through manoeuvres without disturbing it. Land-boat sessions plus intermittent conditioning and a few well-chosen strength staples will get you in good shape in addition to sailing blocks.

The Harness

There are two broad styles of harness: seat ('nappy') and adjustable wrap. Seat harnesses tend to suit a more upright trapeze stance (common in Contenders and some skiffs), while wrap styles offer more tuning for a flatter body line and different pelvic / waist shapes (useful in boats like the 470 and 49er / FX). Choose the style that matches how you typically stand on the wire and where you feel pressure at the hips and pubic bone.

Back support and comfort: Many harnesses use movable pads or vertical battens to spread load across the lower and mid back. Check that the back panel stays put under load; if it rides up, your effective hook height creeps higher and comfort drops.

What to look for when fitting:

- **Snug hips:** Firm, even contact without pinching
- **Spreader bar:** A wider bar distributes load better and reduces hip pinch; side adjusters help you trim stance between upwind / downwind or days with different wind strengths
- A bigger gap between the tip of the hook and the harness allows more room for error when hooking up
- **Leg-strap geometry:** Enough adjustment to keep straps flat on the thigh and out of the groin; avoid pressure on the inner (inguinal) area
- **Adjustability:** Independent, symmetrical adjusters on each side of the hook; quick tweaks are valuable afloat
- **Shoulder interface:** Straps long enough to sit over your buoyancy aid (PFD) and layers; keep the shoulder area smooth and low-bulk to prevent rubbing
- **Back battens / padding:** Built-in support that doesn't shift, plus easy access to rinse and dry after sailing
- **Varied clothing fit:** Re-check fit with winter layers; extra thickness can change hook height by a centimetre or two

Hook position: Set the hook so it sits slightly below the navel. Lower placement supports the pelvis; too high increases lumbar load. Re-check height after any adjustments or clothing changes.

Harness Fit

The trapeze harness often goes on the outside of all clothing, although wearing a rash vest over the top helps keep everything streamlined. Step in and pull the harness up. Throw the shoulder strap over and fasten tight so that the shoulders have to be slightly hunched. This ensures a good fit, as the harness will ride up when you're first on the wire.

The trapeze harness should be sufficiently tight between the groin and shoulders so that the trunk and shoulders are supported when flat-out. If the harness is not tight enough you may find that the core muscles are a little more tired at the end of the day and your shoulders are sore.

The straps attached to the spreader bar should be firm so that, once on the trapeze, the distance between your

The fit of the harness over the shoulders and around the hips is vital for comfortable trapezing

tummy and the hook is minimal – not more than 10cm (4 inches). With the hook in a consistent position in relation to your body you will develop a feel for its position and hook and unhook without looking.

Tuck in all the harness straps so they don't flap around or catch on the rigging. However, you may like to leave the shoulder strap adjustable so you can loosen the load if the wind goes light and you're stuck inboard. Anyway, more often than not, you will need to re-adjust the harness soon after you first hit the wire for a better fit, usually by tightening the shoulder strap.

Trapezing Technique

When you're still getting used to trapezing you struggle to find a balance between stability (feet wide apart) and maximum righting moment (feet together, toes pointed, body flat). With experience in the boat's movement and practice you will gain confidence in your position and get your feet closer together.

Trapezing high, with your feet flat on the deck and legs bent at 90 degrees

It is important to be able to adjust the height at which you trapeze. As a rough guide, the lowest you want the boat's trapeze rings is at the level of the gunwale when measured next to the gunwale. At its highest, you will be trapezing with your feet flat on the deck, legs bent at 90 degrees – as though you are sitting in a chair.

In light winds you won't hit the wire, but avoid taking the harness off – you never know! Loosen the shoulder straps and try not to get the hook caught on anything!

In moderate winds trapeze higher. This way you can swing out from crouching on the deck to fully extended with ease, but not generate so much righting moment that you will pull the boat too far over.

Once the wind is strong enough that you can trapeze all the time, go much lower on the wire. It is important to keep the shoulders back and the legs straight. Get used to looking around at the water, other boats, etc. from this strange angle. For maximum leverage, point the toes and keep a spare arm above your head, if you don't have too much on!

You need to keep your weight out there consistently. You can't get out any further, so you really just have to hang there and provide a consistent righting moment.

You also have a good vantage point from your position on the trapeze and so should feed information back to the helm on wind, waves and competitors.

Tacking

When you hear the call of 'ready about', 'ok', 'let's go' or 'ya right?' you can either unhook while still out there or move in a little, then unhook. You may like to brush your other hand down to make sure the hook is cleared. As the boat flattens and turns through the wind, bend your knees to move in and through the boat.

Try to get out on the new tack as quickly as possible, hanging from the handle and then hooking on when ready.

Of course, this technique varies on different boats. For example, 49er sailors don't unhook until they're halfway in because they will stand upright during the tack – the ring usually falls off. Some sailors have become used to propping on the side deck and hooking up, others prefer to go straight out and then hook up. Nonetheless, when the wind is in, it's ideal to get fully out as soon as possible, so practise hanging from the handle with one arm and then hooking up without looking.

Wire-To-Wire Tack (Taken from *Crewing To Win* by Saskia Clark)

1. From trapezing at maximum leverage, drop the jibsheet behind you

2. With your weight on your front arm, knock the trapeze hoop from your harness and start to come in as the helm steers into the tack

3. As you sit on the side deck, locate your back hand on the working jibsheet and have your front hand ready on the jibsheet near your knees

4. As you go through head to wind, uncleat the old jibsheet and grip the new sheet

5. Duck for the boom, stand up pulling the jibsheet with you and aim your new front hand to the windward trapeze handle

6. Spring from the centreboard case or floor straight onto the gunwale

7. Trim the jib to about right

8. Clip onto the trapeze and fine tune the jib

9. Resume trapezing

Advanced Techniques

In marginal trapezing conditions crews may like to trapeze with their feet on the centreboard case or mast so they're on the wire earlier, ready to slide out with an increase in wind. It also means you can react more subtly to the wind and effectively trim the boat via small movements forward, back, in and out.

Trapezing off the centreboard

On a fresh beat, work hard at making sure your shoulders are back at the tops of waves to help keep the boat flat and accelerate down the back of waves. You need to be quite low on the trapeze in these conditions to maximise your leverage. This makes it a little more difficult to get inboard for a tack, so you could adjust yourself up a little just before the tack. Don't lower yourself so far that you're skimming more than 1 in 20 or so waves with your back. Raise yourself for the downwinds when less righting moment is needed.

The trapeze allows the crew to quickly move forward and backward along the gunwale, especially when sailing downwind. You should take advantage of this to adjust the fore and aft trim of the hull – move forward to keep the stern from dragging and shuffle back to lift the bow and crack the boat onto the plane. It's also a good idea to move backwards when rounding the top mark and on tight reaches (or when ducking a boat) to reduce the chance of the rudder cavitating and the bow digging in.

Small movements on the trapeze are especially beneficial when sailing in waves. You can do some little pushes backward through your feet to help nudge the boat down waves on reaches and runs. These pushes, combined with moving in or out on the trapeze, can do much to help the helmsman trim and steer the boat, reducing his or her need to work hard with the rudder. However, the timing of these movements is critical, and much practice is needed to coordinate them effectively with the wind, waves and your helm.

In big winds and waves your body and / or feet can be slammed by a big wave, and you risk getting washed off the gunwale. Falling sideways into the gunwale or helm is slow! There are a few ways to save you this embarrassment:

- Try trapezing slightly higher
- Let the helm know what's coming in the next boat length or three so that he or she can slightly heel the boat briefly to get you both higher above the waves
- Lock one foot flat against the gunwale for a better grip. Or lift one leg off briefly to avoid the wave
- Use the sheet to brace yourself
- Grab the trapeze rope and pull it sharply towards your head to pull yourself up for a moment
- Do a quick 'bum lift' to avoid a wave heading straight for your behind

Once you've mastered the basics of moving efficiently around the boat and getting on and off the trapeze, you can begin to explore more advanced trapezing techniques. Crews can then experiment with making small, precise movements that help fine-tune balance and increase boatspeed. As these skills become more automatic, you'll also be better placed to use your prime position out on the wire to feed valuable, real-time information back to the helm.

Windsurfing, Winging & Kiting

Windsurfing, winging and kiting each place slightly different demands on the body, but they all share one key theme: staying stable on an unstable platform while controlling a sail, wing or kite that can move and load the body in many directions. Whether pumping a rig, driving through the foil or managing power through the kite or wing, performance depends on how well the legs, trunk and upper body work together to transfer force effectively. This chapter outlines the main physical demands of each discipline and highlights training priorities to support performance on the water.

Windsurfing (non-foiling)

Windsurfing evolved into an endurance-power sport once pumping became an essential skill. In lighter winds, effective pumping allows you to get planing earlier, launch quickly off the line and maintain speed through lulls. In windier conditions, pumping can also be beneficial as a short-term sprint option to gain a tactical advantage. Once you've broken clear, ease back from maximum effort and settle into a more sustainable rhythm, alternating between bursts of pumping and steady, efficient sailing while hooked in.

The resurrected Windsurfer LT (one-design) class permits some pumping but within defined limits. From a fitness perspective the key limiters and areas to target in a typical 20-25-minute course race include:

- **Forearm / grip fatigue:** Try to release or change your grip on the boom every so often and make full use of your harness to lighten the load on your arms
- **Off-the-water training:** Include forearm endurance work and varied-grip pulling (e.g. ***towel dead-hang*** (E4), ***seated row*** (E3) and ***lat pull-down*** (E1) variations)
- **Trunk stability:** Sailboarders effectively balance between four points during manoeuvres – two feet and two hands, but mostly by the feet. This leaves a lot of the body in between. Like an unstayed mast, the body will not be supported properly unless there are strong 'side stays'. Therefore, particular attention should be paid to the lower back and core muscles that stabilise the trunk. Once these areas are strong, your ability to transfer power from the legs and trunk through to the arms and to the sail will increase. Build up exercises involving anti-extension / anti-rotation (***dead bug*** (H3) progressions, ***Pallof presses*** (A15), ***farmer's carries*** (H7)) so leg and hip power transfers cleanly to the rig
- **Shoulders and upper back:** These areas can be uncomfortable because you're pulling at the boom with extended arms and shoulders and this is not a natural position. An exercise like ***scapular retraction*** (E3) can strengthen the muscles in the upper back and keep your shoulders in a good functional position
- **Cross-training:** Activities like indoor rock climbing can also be excellent for building back and shoulder strength, grip endurance, balance and agility – all valuable for windsurfers

With pumping, windsurfing is an endurance-power sport

Windsurfing (Foiling)

Foiling reduces drag, but it also raises the demands on balance, control and timing. Pumping is no longer just about driving the sail. It also involves using the legs and body to transfer energy precisely through the board to the foil. The small contact area between foils and water means that small errors in trim, balance or timing can have a bigger effect on speed and efficiency. This increases the demand for fine control through the ankles, knees, hips and trunk, as the sailor makes constant subtle adjustments to keep the board flying at a consistent ride height.

In practice, this means the athlete must be able to produce force without losing posture or rhythm. Power matters, but so does the ability to apply it smoothly and at the right moment. The sailor needs enough lower-body sensitivity and control to feel and guide the foils, while also staying relaxed enough to respond to changes in wind pressure and direction. Windsurf foiling therefore rewards athletes who can blend strength, timing and body awareness, rather than relying on brute effort alone. As with other disciplines of the sport, it makes sense that spending a good amount of time on the water is vital for skill acquisition and specific fitness development.

For off-water fitness work, in the context of a typical iQFOiL course race of 15-18 minutes, the main priorities include:

- **Core and hips:** Develop anti-rotation and lateral hip strength to control roll, yaw and body position while foiling. ***Copenhagen planks*** (H5), ***wood chop*** (A14), ***farmer's carries*** (H7) and similar exercises help build the strength needed to connect the lower body to the board while keeping movements controlled
- **Ankles and feet:** Train fine pitch and roll control through the feet and lower legs. ***Single-leg balance with perturbations*** (D9), ***calf endurance*** (D10) and ***partial-knee-bend isometrics*** (D9) can help improve stability and the ability to make small corrections without overreacting
- **Repeat surges:** Incorporate 30-60 second intervals with equal rest into aerobic sessions to simulate periods of pumping while getting on the foil, during starts, laylines and mark exits. The aim is not just to produce power once, but to repeat quality efforts while maintaining technique and board control

Foiling increases demands on stability and control

Wing Foiling

Wing foiling combines the challenge of balancing on a fast, unstable foil board with controlling a wing that is free to move independently. Without a rigid link between the board and the power source the rider must generate and manage speed through body position, wing trim and, at times, repeated pumping of wing and board. This creates a strong demand for coordination and whole-body control, especially through the trunk, hips and shoulders.

Most beginners quickly notice how much the core is involved. That does not disappear as skill improves. What changes is the precision of the control. More experienced riders are still working to stay stable, but with small, well-timed adjustments through the feet, hips and trunk, and are better at keeping the wing in an efficient relationship to the board and body. This matters not only during active pumping phases, but also during steadier sections of racing when the rider is trying to stay fast and balanced without wasting energy.

Wing foiling therefore places a premium on trunk

endurance, hip stability and lower-leg control, together with enough upper-body strength and grip endurance to manage the wing effectively. The better riders often make the hard work look tidy. They absorb changes in pressure more cleanly and keep the board moving without obvious tension or unnecessary movement.

In a typical 6-8-minute race, the main fitness priorities are:

- **Grip and shoulders:** In the gym, combine static holds and movement-based strength, such as ***farmer's carries*** (H7) and ***seated rows*** (E3), to build grip endurance, shoulder strength and the ability to maintain control of the wing. Change hand positions often
- **Core and balance:** Focus on resisting twists and side bends while maintaining good ankle and hip control. ***Pallof presses*** (A15), ***Copenhagen planks*** (H5) and ***single-leg balance drills*** (D9) work well here, helping the rider stay connected and stable while the wing and foil are both creating movement
- **Endurance and bursts:** Combine steady aerobic efforts for both legs and arms with short, high-intensity bursts. Practise quick starts, repeated accelerations and hitting optimal VMG out of marks, while maintaining posture and coordination under fatigue

Wing foiling has specific fitness requirements

Kite Foiling

Kite foiling has a different physical profile from winging and windsurfing because the athlete is always connected to the kite through the harness, and the geometry of the forces involved is very different. This changes how force is transferred through the body. Although the harness can reduce some of the constant arm loading seen in other board disciplines, it does not make the event physically easy. Instead, much of the demand shifts toward lower-body strength endurance, trunk rigidity and the ability to control ride height and direction accurately at speed.

A defining feature of kite foiling is the squat position adopted while riding fast under load. Holding this position well requires strength and endurance through the hips and thighs, especially in the gluteals and quadriceps. Stronger legs help the rider maintain posture, absorb force and stay effective through gusts, chop and changes in angle. For this reason, lower body strength training has clear value in kite foiling, not only for peak force production, but also for improving the rider's ability to hold efficient positions for longer and with less fatigue.

As performance level rises, the event becomes less about simply coping with the load and more about handling it with precision. Better riders are typically more economical in how they manage kite load via body position and board / foil trim, but that economy still rests on a strong lower-body base.

In a typical race, the main fitness priorities are:

- **Leg and hip strength:** Develop the strength to hold an effective squat position under load and maintain posture at speed. Exercises such as ***squats*** (D3), ***split squats*** (D3), ***step-ups*** (D4) and ***deadlift variations*** (D5) help build the gluteal, quadriceps, hamstring and back strength needed for both force production and position holding
- **Core connection:** Focus on transmitting force between the harness, trunk and board while resisting unwanted rotation and side-bending. ***Pallof presses*** (A15), ***farmer's carries*** (H7) and ***wood chops*** (A14) can help develop this connection
- **Lower-leg and board control:** Train ankle stability, balance and fine control so small adjustments can be made without excessive tension. ***Single-leg balance drills*** (D9) and ***calf endurance work*** (D10) are useful here

- **Repeatability:** Combine aerobic work with repeated race-like surges and longer loaded efforts. The goal is to maintain posture, precision and decision-making quality late in races and across a series

Kite foiling requires lower-body strength endurance

Shared 'Board Athlete' Principles

Regardless of whether it is windsurfing, winging or kite foiling, board sports share several important training themes. All three reward athletes who can create force while staying stable, connected and adaptable on an unstable platform. In practice, that means not just being strong, but being able to apply strength in useful positions, at the right time and with enough control to keep the board moving efficiently.

Another shared feature is the constant need to organise the body against changing external load from wind and wave pressure. Athletes therefore need the very practical sort of strength that works in real movement, not just in isolated gym exercises. They also need balance that holds up when pulling, pushing, rotating or absorbing force, rather than balance trained only in quiet, passive positions.

Across all board disciplines, it also makes sense to think in terms of progression. First, build general strength and movement quality. Then develop power and speed. After that, train the ability to repeat those efforts with good technique under fatigue. This helps ensure that gym work supports what matters most on the water: being able to stay fast, effective and coordinated from the first important effort to the last.

- **Specificity first:** The best training is still time on the water. Build sessions around real race moments such as starts, pumps, lulls and mark roundings, rather than random fitness work
- **Strength → power → repeatability:** Start with general strength (squat, push, pull, carry), then build speed and power (jumps, throws or lighter lifts), and finally train the ability to repeat those efforts under fatigue
- **Balance under load:** Train balance in ways that still involve pulling, pushing, rotating or absorbing load. The goal is to stay stable while producing force, not just to balance in passive positions
- **Shoulder control and posture:** Lead each pull with your shoulder blades. Think 'blades down and back, neck long, move smooth'. This helps keep the shoulders strong and pain-free
- **Daily small stuff:** Spend 5-10 minutes on hips, ankles and upper-back mobility. These small habits help you move better and avoid little injuries
- **In-season maintenance:** One or two short gym sessions a week is enough to hold strength. Keep it simple: a few key exercises done well

Here's a simple example land endurance session (30-35 minutes) that would suit all of the board disciplines:

- 5-minute warm-up
- 2,000m ergometer row
- 40-50 core / trunk reps (***sit-up to stand*** (A1) / ***dead bug*** (H3) mix)
- 30-40 ***body pull-ups*** (E5) (broken sets)
- 2,000m ergometer row
- Easy spin + mobility

PART 3

TRAINING

Time Budgeting: Getting The Best Return On Each Hour

One training day, I left shore with Australian Gold medallist Tom King working on his 470 – tools, parts, rope and tape everywhere. When I returned about four hours later, he was still at it. I had seen similar scenes day after day and asked him why he didn't get more on-the-water time. He reckoned that there was a 470 class rule that you needed to do three hours of boat work for every one hour on the water. He was getting ready to sail overseas so he had to get his boat work hours up!

In practice, Tom got ample on-the-water time in a very well-prepared boat and, despite my relative lack of Laser boat work, I rarely had any breakdowns on the water. It showed me how important allocating the right amount of time to the many aspects of your preparation can be – fitness, boat maintenance, equipment selection, weather, psychology and rules.

In the simple one-design single-handed classes such as ILCA and iQFOiL, physical training on-shore or on-the-water will make up a larger portion of total training time because less boat work is needed.

On the 470, 49er and Nacra, fitness is still important but because the boats are inherently more complicated, including sail and mast combinations, ropes and foils, proportionally more time should go to obtaining and testing equipment that can make the boat go faster.

At the far end of the spectrum, America's Cup design teams spend an enormous amount of time designing and tuning boats and rigs (while the sailing teams hit the gym waiting for their new equipment to be readied!).

So, opposite are some figures to illustrate where the priorities might lie for each class. You can see that all classes have the same general emphasis on Boatspeed and Racing Skills (starting, strategy and tactics). While Fitness is its own area, it also contributes to Boatspeed and can impact the quality of the decision making that's a part of your Racing Skills. There are other crossovers too, for example, Fitness will influence Boat Handling, say, a spinnaker hoist or recovery from a capsize.

Of course, this is only my rough guide as to how much of your available time you should spend in each area. You should also consider your own strengths and weaknesses. For example, if you are unfit, but can trim a boat well and pick shifts easily, you can allocate more time to physical training.

You can also see by the chart that I suggest that a 49er crew should spend about 30% of the time they devote to sailing on improving their boat's speed. Rig settings, sail and hull trim and fitness all influence boatspeed, so they contribute to this 30% as well.

This time allocation is slightly less than a 470 crew because the 49er is more of a true one-design class while the 470 allows a number of sailmakers in the class. Kite, wing and iQFOiL sailors may like to spend more time on some form of psychology work, to prepare for back-to-back split-second decisions that need to be made at high speed.

Create your own chart – tailored to your class – like the one opposite. Start by honestly assessing your strengths and weaknesses, then allocate your training time accordingly. Be specific to where you are now and what you need to improve before the next major event.

Where to spend training time

Suggested percentage time to be spent on each facet of sailboat racing by class. Note: Racing Skills = starting, strategy and tactics

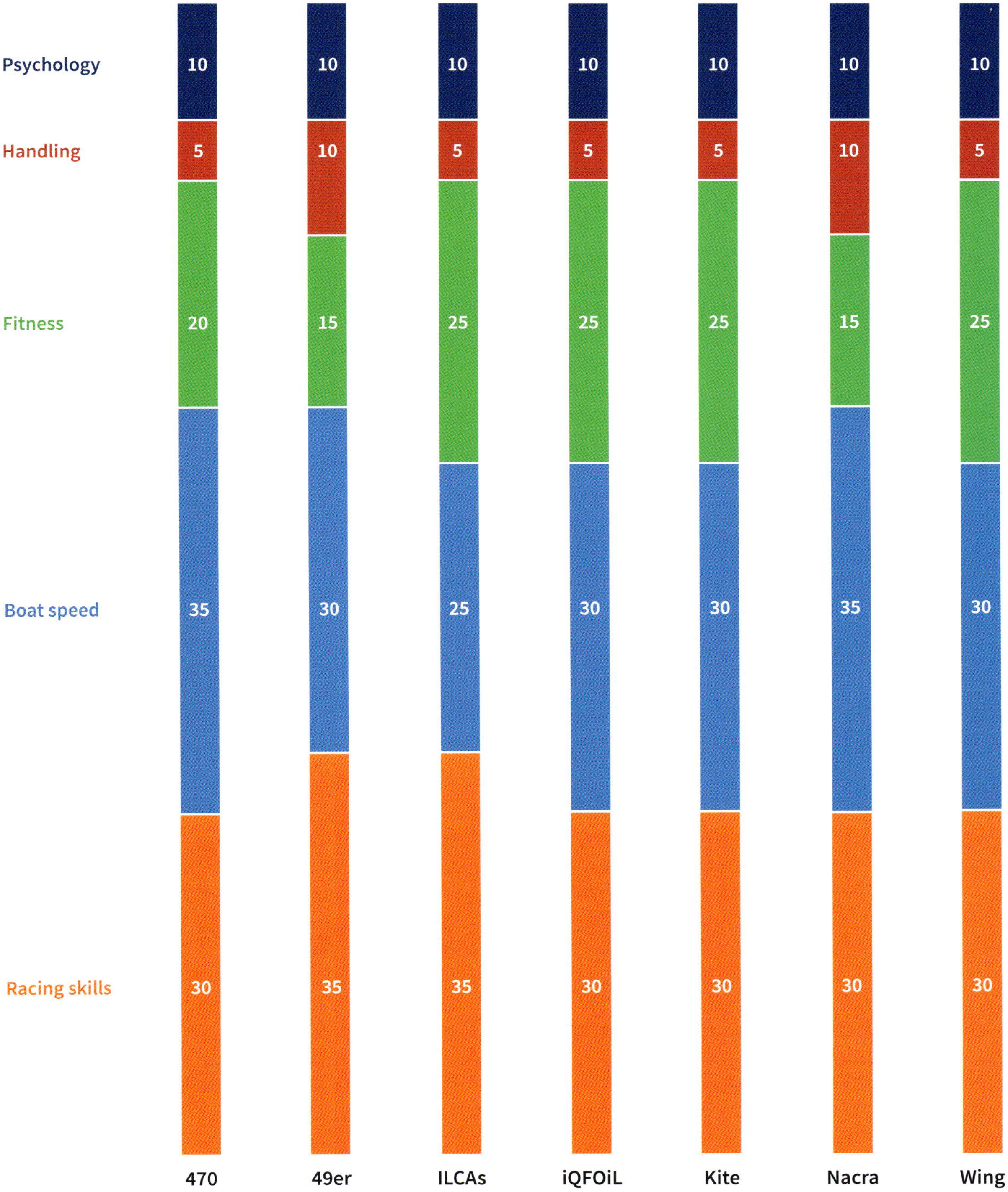

Top Seven Training Sessions

In this chapter are some of my favourite high-quality training sessions that improve sailing performance, counting down from 7 to 1 – increasing in importance. Use these as a guide to the types of activities that can be done on a daily basis. Having a repertoire of sessions that you are happy to do ensures quality and variety in your training and encourages you to stick to your training programme.

For more details of the specific exercises, and full photo sequences, see the appendix.

Getting Started: Building Your Training Foundation

Before jumping into the top sessions, it's important to know where to begin. If you're new to structured training or haven't trained consistently for a while, start by building a general fitness base before tackling the full version of these sessions. Sailing is demanding – physically, mentally and technically – so your first goal should be to establish consistency, not intensity.

Start with aerobic conditioning (cycling, running or swimming 3-4 times a week for 20-40 minutes), mobility work for hips and shoulders and basic core control exercises. Once you can comfortably complete moderate aerobic sessions and some simple strength work, add one or two of the 'Top Seven Sessions' each week. Over time, progress by increasing session duration or load gradually – not all at once.

A simple eight-week outline might look like this:

- **Weeks 1-2:** Light aerobic activity and mobility drills
- **Weeks 3-4:** Add core work (***crunches*** (A2), ***reverse sit-ups*** (A10)) and light bodyweight strength (***gym ball*** (B), ***chin-ups*** (E2))
- **Weeks 5-8:** Introduce endurance or resistance-based sessions (bike intervals, hiking bench, weights)
- **Beyond:** Combine sessions to maintain balance, variety and motivation

Keep a basic log of what you do – a smart watch and apps like TrainingPeaks, Garmin Connect or Strava can help you track effort, recovery and progress.

No.7: Postural / Hiking Muscles: Crunch & Reverse Sit-Ups

This session is a simple example of a dedicated core workout – one that targets the muscles responsible for stabilising the trunk and supporting movement and good posture on the water. A strong, well-conditioned core helps prevent low-back pain and allows you to maintain efficient body positions for longer periods when hiking, trapezing or windsurfing.

In practice, these exercises are often interspersed within other sessions rather than performed alone – for example, between sets in a gym programme or tagged onto the end of a strength or endurance session. This flexible approach makes it easier to train the core frequently without adding excessive time or fatigue to your weekly program. Whether you're an ILCA sailor, 49er crew or foiling board sailor, regular core training underpins your ability to move efficiently, stay balanced and control power through the rig in variable conditions.

Warm-Up
5-10 minutes of light aerobic activity (e.g. jogging, skipping, cycling) followed by gentle stretching for the hips, hamstrings and lower back.

Exercise 1: *Crunch* (A2)
What To Do: Lie on your back with knees bent and feet flat on the floor. Cross your arms over your chest or place fingertips lightly behind your ears. Engage your core and lift your shoulders and upper back off the floor. Keep the lower back pressed into the ground throughout.
Repetitions: 4-5 sets of 10-20 controlled repetitions. Hold the top position for 2 seconds before lowering slowly. Move up quickly, down slowly.

Advanced Level: Add resistance by holding a small weight plate or medicine ball on your chest or perform on an incline bench. Avoid pulling the neck or using momentum.

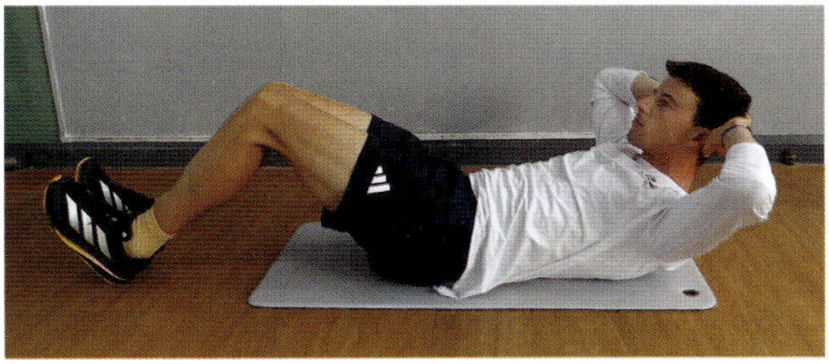

Crunch: A partial sit-up in which you lift the trunk, but not the lower back, off the floor. The hip flexor muscles are not involved

Exercise 2: *Reverse Sit-Up* (A10)
What To Do: Lie flat on your back with knees slightly bent. Keeping shoulders relaxed, lift both feet up and roll the hips to raise your feet toward or over your head. Lower legs slowly until heels are just above the ground and repeat.

Repetitions: 4-5 sets of 10-20 repetitions, interspersed between other exercises or used during rest breaks in a gym session.

Advanced Level: Once 30 repetitions feel easy, progress to harder variations from the Appendix (e.g. ***hanging knee raises*** (A13) and ***V-sits*** (A11)).

Reverse sit-up: Lay flat on ground, knees slightly bent. Lift both feet up and well over your head and lower to just above the ground

Exercise 3: *Dead Bug* (H3)
What to Do: Lie on your back with arms extended toward the ceiling and knees bent at 90°. Engage your core so your lower back stays gently pressed into the floor. Slowly lower one arm and the opposite leg towards the ground while keeping the other arm and leg still. Return to the start and alternate sides.

Repetitions: 3-4 sets of 8-12 controlled reps per side. Each repetition should take 4-6 seconds total – control is more important than range.

Dead Bug: Lay on your back with arms extended to the ceiling and knees bent at 90°. Engage your core and slowly lower one arm and lower leg towards the ground

Advanced Level: Hold small weights in your hands or use resistance bands around the feet. For added challenge, extend both legs simultaneously (advanced sailors only – this is demanding on the lower back).

Post-Training / Warm Down
Stretch the lower back, glutes, hip flexors and hamstrings, and add gentle lumbar rotations. Finish with gentle spinal rotations to release tension.

Progression Notes
After several weeks of consistent work, introduce one or two advanced core variations per session. There's no need to do them all at once – variety keeps the routine fresh and helps target the core from different angles.

No.6: Hiking & Sheeting Endurance: Gym Ball Hiking Leg Extensions & Body-Weight Pull-Ups

This session targets the leg, hip and upper-body endurance needed to hold hiking and sheeting positions for long periods – especially in dinghy sailing, trapezing and other small boat classes. It's simple, portable and ideal when you're travelling or training away from home, requiring only minimal equipment.

You can perform it as a stand-alone circuit or tag it onto the end of a gym session for 15-30 minutes of specific muscular endurance work.

Warm-Up
5-10 minutes of light aerobic activity such as jogging, skipping or cycling, followed by hip, hamstring and shoulder mobility stretches.

Exercise 1: ***Gym Ball Hiking Leg Extensions*** **(D6)**
What To Do: Choose a gym ball that suits your height (55cm if shorter, 65cm if taller). Sit on the ball, anchor your feet under something solid – a couch, bed or dumbbell rack – and push the ball forward under you until your knees are roughly over the top of the ball. Lean back a little so you're close to a normal hiking position. From there, the task is simply to straighten and bend your legs, primarily working the quads. Maintain tension in the core throughout.
Repetitions: Up to 120 extensions total, broken into mini sets of 20 with 5 seconds rest between each.
Advanced Level: Lean your trunk slightly further back to increase resistance or add a small weight plate held to the chest. Maintain form – avoid bouncing on the ball, leaning too far back or over-extending through the lower back.
Post-Training / Warm Down: Stretch hip flexors, quadriceps and lower back. Finish with gentle spinal extensions to relieve pressure from the hiking position.

Hiking leg extensions on the gym ball: Lean your trunk back a little for added resistance

Exercise 2: ***Body-Weight Pull-Up (Horizontal Row)*** **(E5)**
What To Do: Lie face-up under the edge of a sturdy table or horizontal bar. Grip the edge or bar with hands about shoulder-width apart and arms nearly straight. Bend your knees around 90°. Pull your chest up to lightly touch the underside of the table or bar, pause briefly, then lower under control.
Repetitions: 4-6 sets of 15-20 repetitions or perform within a timed circuit (see below).

Keep the movement smooth – focus on shoulder-blade engagement rather than arm pulling alone.

Body weight pull-up: Lie under a horizontal bar. Pull your chest up to lightly touch the underside of the bar, pause briefly, then lower under control

Advanced Level: Elevate your feet on a chair for greater resistance or wear a light backpack for extra load.
Post-Training / Warm Down: Stretch the lats, shoulders and chest. Include gentle thoracic rotations and shoulder rolls to relax the upper back.

Suggested Circuit Format
Duration: 20 minutes (adaptable from 10-30 minutes depending on fitness).

Example Rotation:

- 2 minutes gym ball ***hiking leg extensions*** (D6)
- 20 ***body-weight pull-ups*** (E5)
- Light rest / transition to next set

Repeat 5 rotations. Each round should take ~4 minutes. Gradually increase the leg-extension count in later rounds for progression.

Progression Notes
Once you can comfortably complete 20 minutes of this circuit, increase difficulty by:

- Adding more mini-sets or reducing rest between them
- Leaning further back on the gym ball
- Performing the body-weight pull-ups with feet elevated

This combination delivers a good simulation of the muscular endurance required for real on-the-water hiking and sheeting – especially valuable during off-water periods or poor weather days.

No.5: Muscle Strength: Weight Training

Upper-body strength is essential for handling ropes, steering, hoisting sails and lifting your boat. The key areas are arms, shoulders, chest and back.

A general principle of weight training is to do fewer repetitions per set (e.g. four sets of 4-10 reps) to build strength and more repetitions per set to develop muscular endurance (e.g. two sets of 15-40 reps).

For sailors in pre-season training, it may be best to do, say, four to eight weeks of strength training followed by six weeks of muscular endurance work. This acts to build muscle strength then uses that strength to enhance the muscles' endurance and get them in the best shape for working the sails.

Goal	Reps & Sets	Phase	Notes
Build Strength	4 × 4-10 reps	Pre-season (5-10 weeks)	Heavier loads, full control
Build Endurance	2 × 15-40 reps	Follow-on (≈ 6 weeks)	Lighter loads, steady rhythm

Start with weights you could lift two more times than prescribed, but no more. If you breeze through the set, it's too light. If your form breaks down before the target reps, it's too heavy. Technique always comes first.

Also, progressively increase the weight you lift over a period of weeks. Improvements in strength and muscle endurance from weight training can only be expected with a minimum of two to three sessions a week, so pay up your gym fees and get to it properly. Otherwise, concentrate on other activities mentioned here.

Sample Strength Session
(After 2-4 weeks of prep work with lighter loads)
Warm-Up: 10 minutes light cardio + shoulder and trunk mobility
Main Work: 4 sets × 4-10 reps with a rest break of 60-90 seconds
Exercises:

- *Bench press* (C2) **or** *Push-ups* (C1)
- *Pull-ups* (E5) or *Lat pull-down* (E1)
- *Seated row* (E3) or *Bench row* (E6)
- *Military press* (G3)
- *Biceps curl* (E10) + *Prone hand walk* (B3)

Session	Intensity	Adjustment
1	Hard	100% (freshest day)
2	Medium	90%
3	Light	80%

Strength Training Weekly Loading: Adjusting the loading as just shown reduces the risk of injury and overtraining, yet it still provides a good enough stimulus to improve your muscles' strength.

Sample Endurance Session
(After strength block completion)
Warm-Up: 10 minutes dynamic stretch + shoulder circles
Main Work: 2 sets × 15-40 reps with a rest break of just 30 seconds
Exercises:

- *Push-ups* (C1) or *Incline bench press* (C2) (light)
- *Band rows* or *Cable rows* (E3)
- *Three-way shoulder work* (G1)
- *Towel grip seated row* (E3) or *Bench rows* (E6)
- Core finisher (*Crucifix* (A9) or *Wood chop* (A14))

Lower Body Add-Ons
Strength and muscular endurance training can also be done for the leg muscles. In particular, the quadriceps can be developed using exercises such as ***leg presses*** (D2), ***squats*** (D3) and ***leg extensions*** (D1).

These can be added to the above sample sessions to improve thigh strength and hiking endurance. However, it may be better to do most of your heavy leg workouts either on the water, on a hiking bench or on a bike. This ensures that the legs are trained specifically for the job they do on the water.

No.4: Endurance: Cycling & Rowing Machine

This session develops aerobic endurance and upper-body stamina – the combination you rely on for sustained hiking and repetitive sheeting during long races. It pairs cycling for leg endurance with rowing-machine 'sheeting' drills that closely mimic the upper-body demands of sailing.

The full circuit takes about one hour, including warm-up and cool-down, and can be modified for shorter sessions when time is limited.

Warm-Up

3 minutes of light pedalling on an exercise bike. Gradually increase intensity until breathing is steady but comfortable and the legs feel warm. Finish with a minute of walking lunges before the main work.

Exercise 1: Cycle Block 1

What To Do: Pedal continuously for 17 minutes, building effort to reach a heart rate of 130-160bpm (moderate → hard effort). Maintain an even cadence.

Repetitions / Duration: 1 × 17-minute effort.

Advanced Level: Add gentle resistance climbs or 60-second surges every 5 minutes to simulate tactical situations and mark roundings.

Post-Block: Dismount and stretch quads and hip flexors for about 1 minute.

Exercise 2: *Rowing-Machine 'Sheeting' Drill* 1 (E9)

What To Do: Sit on the rowing machine with legs almost straight and lightly flexed knees. Set the resistance low – on a Concept 2 rower, pull the lever to 0. Pull the handle with one arm at a time, alternating left and right to mirror the mainsheet action. Each pull should finish with a firm shoulder-blade squeeze.

Repetitions / Duration: 6 minutes total. Start light for 1 minute, then perform 6 strong pulls per arm at ~85 % effort, alternating sides over the 6 minutes.

Advanced Level: Use higher drag factor or stronger resistance for short bursts; maintain correct posture without twisting.

Post-Block: Stretch forearms and shoulders; shake out arms for 30 seconds.

'Sheeting' on a rowing machine: A great simulation of on-the-water action

Exercise 3: Cycle Block 2

What To Do: Return to the bike for another 20 minutes of steady aerobic work at a similar or slightly higher intensity than the first block.

Repetitions / Duration: 1 × 20-minute effort. Include short cadence variations (30-second high-spin bursts every 5 minutes).

Advanced Level: Insert short periods out of the saddle or up the resistance to push the power output higher.

Post-Block: Take a 2-minute easy spin before moving to the final rowing set.

Exercise 4: *Rowing-Machine 'Sheeting' Drill* 2 (E9)

What To Do: Repeat the earlier sheeting sequence for another 6 minutes, focusing on smooth rhythm and consistent pull strength. Visualise the motion of trimming a sail through gusts or mark roundings.

Advanced Level: Finish each minute with 10 more powerful pulls while keeping form controlled.

Cool-Down

5 minutes of easy cycling or light rowing to bring the heart rate down, followed by leg, shoulder and back stretches.

Session Summary / Timing Guide

Segment	Duration	Focus
Warm-Up	3 minutes	Gentle spin
Cycle Block 1	17 minutes	Build aerobic effort
Sheeting Drill 1	6 minutes	Upper-body power
Short Break	2 minutes	Stretch / reset
Cycle Block 2	20 minutes	Endurance
Sheeting Drill 2	6 minutes	Repeat sheeting action
Cool-Down	5 minutes	Recovery

Progression Notes

Repeat this workout 1-2 times per week in the pre-season. As endurance improves, lengthen the cycling phases, shorten the breaks or add a third sheeting block. Aim to maintain steady breathing and posture throughout – the hallmark of on-the-water fitness.

No.3: Endurance: Cycling

Cycling is one of the most effective ways to develop aerobic endurance, leg strength and circulation – three qualities that translate really well to better sailing performance. It's also accessible, joint-friendly and easy to adapt to different training phases or schedules.

For many sailors, especially juniors, simply riding to school or training 10-20 minutes each way at an easy pace builds a strong foundation. As fitness improves, structured rides can replace or complement on-the-water endurance sessions.

Warm-Up: 5-10 minutes of easy pedalling, gradually increasing cadence and effort until breathing is steady and you're slightly sweaty.

Advanced Level: Add short accelerations every 5-10 minutes (10-20 seconds) or include short hill climbs to simulate bursts of activity on the start line or tactical situations. Use a bike computer or heart rate monitor to track loading.

Post-Training / Warm Down: 5-10 minutes of light pedalling followed by gentle stretching for quads, hamstrings, calves and lower back.

Training Notes

- A comfortable, well-fitted bike is very nice to have – you'll ride more often and recover better
- Combine cycling with upper-body or core work 2-3 times a week for balance
- For wet or cold conditions, indoor trainers or smart bikes are excellent alternatives

Progression Notes

Start with short, low intensity rides several times per week. Over a few weeks, increase duration first, then intensity. Build towards completing one longer ride each week at a steady effort comparable to the length of a typical race day, or up to 2 hours.

Cycling Session Options

Type	Duration	Intensity	Description
Long-Slow Endurance	90+ mins	Moderate	Continuous ride to build base aerobic capacity. Keep cadence steady & breathing comfortable
Moderate Aerobic	45-75 mins	Moderate – High	Continuous effort simulating a long upwind leg – smooth but purposeful pedalling
Heavy Aerobic / Interval Hills	~45 mins	High (with rests)	Alternating hard hill efforts & recovery spins on flat sections or back down the hill. Mimics race intensity efforts

No.2: The Simulator: Hiking Bench & Land Boat Training

When it's too windy, not windy enough or just too cold, you can still get meaningful sailing-specific work done through simulator sessions. These dry-land workouts replicate on-the-water demands, maintaining hiking fitness, boat-handling movement patterns and mental engagement. They're ideal when travel, weather or equipment issues prevent normal training – and they also allow controlled repetition of sailing movements in a way that's hard to achieve on the water.

Warm-Up

5-10 minutes of light aerobic work such as a short jog, bike ride or skipping to raise body temperature. Follow with dynamic stretches for hips, hamstrings and shoulders.

Exercise 1: Hiking Bench Session

It's not hard to make yourself a hiking bench out of wood and appropriate designs can be found on class websites. Alternatively, just measure the dimensions of your boat, particularly the distance from the hiking strap to the gunwale. Use heavy screws or bolts to secure the pieces together because you'll be placing quite a load on the bench, as you get fitter.

What To Do: Hike on your bench (or gym ball) in as close to a typical position as you can. Stay in hiking mode (on and off) for 10-30 minutes or longer to match race duration.

Add variety to maintain focus:

- Watch sailing videos of yourself and mimic the timing and movements
- Use a shock-cord mainsheet and a tiller extension to simulate sheeting and steering actions
- Insert 'tacks' periodically – stand up, reset and re-hike – to break the position and reset posture
- Alternatively, listen to music or a podcast to sustain engagement for longer sessions

Repetitions / Duration: 10-30 minutes interval-based (e.g. 10 x 2-minute hiking bouts with 20 second rests).

Advanced Level: Add measurement of effort using a 'Hike-O-Matic' (see below). Track time under tension and aim to increase duration or resistance gradually over time.

Post-Training / Warm Down: Stretch hip flexors, hamstrings and lower back. Add gentle spinal rotations or a short walk to loosen up after static holds.

Exercise 2: Hike-O-Matic Enhancement

What To Do: Upgrade your bench by adding a round bar under the main frame, perpendicular to the bench. This allows the set-up to rock backward when you apply enough hiking force, turning it into a mini seesaw. Mark different resistance positions on the bench so you can move the bar in or out to track intensity. Use this to measure progress and to keep your hiking efforts 'honest'.

Advanced Level: Test yourself by seeing how long you can hold a particular level.

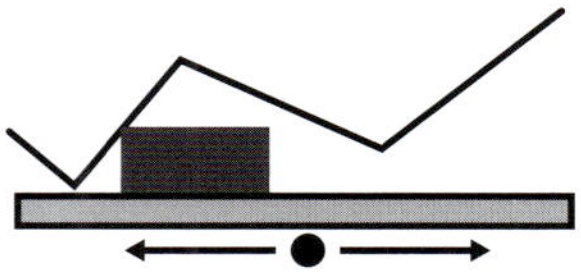

Use the 'Hike-o-Matic' to make your hiking sessions measurable and honest

Exercise 3: Land-Boat Handling Drill (For Crews Or Two-Handed Classes)

What To Do: If you sail a double-handed boat, rig your boat securely on its trolley or trailer and practise movement patterns:

- Simulate tacks, gybes and spinnaker sets with ropes tensioned using shock-cord
- Focus on precision of hand and foot placement
- Repeat sequences to build rhythm and consistency

Repetitions / Duration: 10-20 minutes, repeating complete manoeuvres as short sets (e.g. 4 tacks, reset, 4 gybes).

Advanced Level: Record your movements on video to enable post-session analysis of effort and technique.

Post-Training / Warm Down: Stretch shoulders, back and hips. Add a few minutes of light rowing or cycling to promote recovery.

Progression Notes

- Begin with short sessions (10-15 minutes total)
- Over several weeks, extend total hiking or movement duration, or add light resistance
- Track time and effort to ensure measurable gains
- Simulator sessions can supplement 1-2 gym or on-the-water sessions per week when conditions prevent sailing

No.1: Sailing

From forty-five minutes to four hours of sailing in winds above 10 knots are ideal for developing sailing fitness. Any less and you've barely earned the time spent rigging; much more and fatigue can begin to erode both learning quality and recovery.

High-Intensity On-The-Water Activities

These sessions should challenge your aerobic and muscular endurance while not ignoring racing skills. Use short, purposeful bouts (1-5 minutes) with similar rest periods to maintain intensity.

Good options include:

- Boatspeed / trim sprints – short, 2-3-minute max-effort upwind efforts focusing on speed, sheeting precision and body position. Work : rest ratio = 2 : 1 (e.g. 2 minutes on / 1 minute easy sail)
- Repeated laps around a short course – 3-4 laps on a 2 minute up / down course without break including mark roundings, tacks and gybes
- Close reaching duels – with higher boatspeed and apparent wind, racing another boat at this angle to the wind can be a solid physical effort
- Long upwind hiking stints – 8-12-minute blocks at race intensity, separated by easy downwinds
- Tight upwind covers – shadow a partner closely, clamping on top of them through multiple tacks, forcing quick reactions, tacking agility and good trim
- Heavier clothing or gear – add a little load through the trunk and shoulders to raise effort levels (avoid overheating in summer!)

When The Wind Eases

If the breeze drops below fitness-building range, you can still create load:

- Turn off ratchet blocks to increase sheeting effort
- No hiking pants or harness (for board sailors) to demand more core engagement
- High-frequency tacking – 10-15m tack intervals in a short match-race against a partner
- Stage races with free pumping / rocking to simulate high-output kinetics

When It's Too Light

If you're ghosting along with minimal resistance, don't waste the time. Paddle back in and move to your simulator, hiking bench or gym ball for targeted dry-land work.

Why On-The-Water Training Wins

On-the-water sailing remains the gold standard for fitness development because the gains are perfectly specific: balance, core endurance, coordination and decision-making all under race stress. The physical benefits are reinforced by the real-world variability of wind, waves and handling. Despite the extra effort of rigging, launching and packing away, the quality of stimulus makes it the most efficient form of conditioning – and it's far more fun.

Session Outline

Warm-Up: Before lifting the boat or board to the water, get the circulation going with light movement and dynamic stretches. For hiking sailors, a walking lunge is great to get blood to the legs and activate the hip flexors. Trapezing and board sailors can spend a minute or two on arm swings, shoulder rolls and band pull-aparts to loosen the shoulders and prime the pulling muscles for action.

Once afloat, ease into the session with 10-15 minutes of semi-hiking, gentle sheeting and steering drills. Then pause for a quick stretch if it feels like anything needs it (hamstrings, hip flexors, thighs, shoulders or lower back) before pushing into higher intensity.

Mid-Session Reset: In long sessions or between races, take a few minutes to stretch and relax the key muscle groups. It helps maintain posture and performance through fatigue

Lower back stretch: Place one foot beside the knee of the opposite leg. With the opposite arm against the bent knee, twist the trunk around

Quadriceps and hip flexor stretch: Start in a kneeling position then reach back with your hand to grab the opposite foot, gently pulling the foot to your bottom. Keep the trunk upright and core tight

Hamstring stretch: Extend one leg straight in front (other leg bent). Slowly reach forward, grasping the ankle or toes for extra leverage

Chest and biceps stretch: Clasp the hands behind the lower back then slowly extend them backwards and upwards

Cool-Down And Recovery: The sail home usually doubles as a low-intensity cool-down. Continue recovery ashore:

- Post-sailing stretch: Warm shower plus 5 minutes of easy mobility work
- Later that day: Re-stretch or self-massage any tight areas
- Next-day prep: Light aerobic movement and another stretch to restore range before racing again

These small habits keep the muscles supple, reduce soreness and make your body feel more ready again the next morning.

Top 7 Session Summary

All intensities and durations of the above sessions can be individualised to your fitness level. The sessions are designed for those who have already completed some background training (especially aerobic exercise). Therefore, untrained sailors should begin with lighter workloads to allow a build-up period. The main point is to give your mind every chance during races by training your body to increase stamina, strength and suppleness so that any suffering and soreness are not a constant distraction to plotting superb strategy and executing terrific tactics.

You do need to push yourself to really improve.

Occasionally, remember to search inside yourself and ask 'what would happen if I pushed myself a little harder? Would it help me achieve my goals?' Also, consider things like 'what would happen if I leant back a little bit further when hiking? Would the boat go faster?'

A good training partner is invaluable in this regard. I've been lucky enough to have good training partners who have made me work harder. Training one week with multi–Gold Medallist Ben Ainslie, we went on a long run together. We started at a moderate pace, chatting and looking over the countryside. Then we turned for home. I increased the pace a little; he responded and increased it a little more. I strode up to match him again. We were a few kilometres from home and I knew I didn't have a good sprint, so I went hard and put a gap between us. I was near maximum effort coming up the last hill, but he was still right on my tail so I pushed hard again through to the finish.

It was a meaningless little run, but each of us benefited by exercising harder than we would alone, through competition. Of course, the same goes on the water.

That kind of drive is essential, but it has to be balanced. It's easy to get caught up in pushing harder and training more, yet that can come at a cost. I've learnt that when I go to the gym early in the morning for a strength session, my body simply isn't ready for maximum effort. I've tried – and ended up with a strain from pushing too hard. Real progress comes from extending your comfort zone safely, using good technique and listening to the signs your body gives you when something isn't quite right.

PART 4

TRAINING IN PRACTICE

Yearly Training

Another season rolls around and it's time to prepare for the year ahead. You've read up on training, sailing and performance, and you know which exercises help you sail fitter and faster. But have you got a plan? You might know what to do, but do you know when to do it?

To make your training count, you need a yearly plan – a simple structure that builds fitness, skills and recovery in the right order so you can hit peak performance when it matters most. This structured approach is called periodisation.

Periodisation is used by coaches and athletes in all top-level sports. It's a professional way to plan and monitor training loads so that performance steadily improves across the year and reaches a high point for the major event. In practice, it means dividing your year into several phases, each defined by the type and intensity of training, and by how close you are to competition.

Since the goal of all training is to perform well at regattas, the first step is to map out your competition calendar. Mark your key events, then work backwards from your main regatta to plan the build-up. The idea is simple:

- Regular training builds fitness
- Recovery allows that fitness to consolidate
- And tapering before a big event reduces fatigue while preserving – and often enhancing – the underlying fitness, allowing a performance boost when it really counts

Regular training creates controlled stress. Each session adds a small load that your body adapts to, making you stronger and more resilient. These gains don't appear instantly – the full benefit of an aerobic or strength session can take several days to show. That's why serious sailors often feel a little fatigued during heavy training periods. You're not meant to be fully fresh all the time; the aim is to accumulate enough stress and recovery cycles to drive improvement.

Because of that ongoing fatigue, you're rarely at peak condition in training. The taper – a period of reduced training before competition – is what allows you to recover, rebuild and hit your highest level just as racing begins.

Yearly training plan

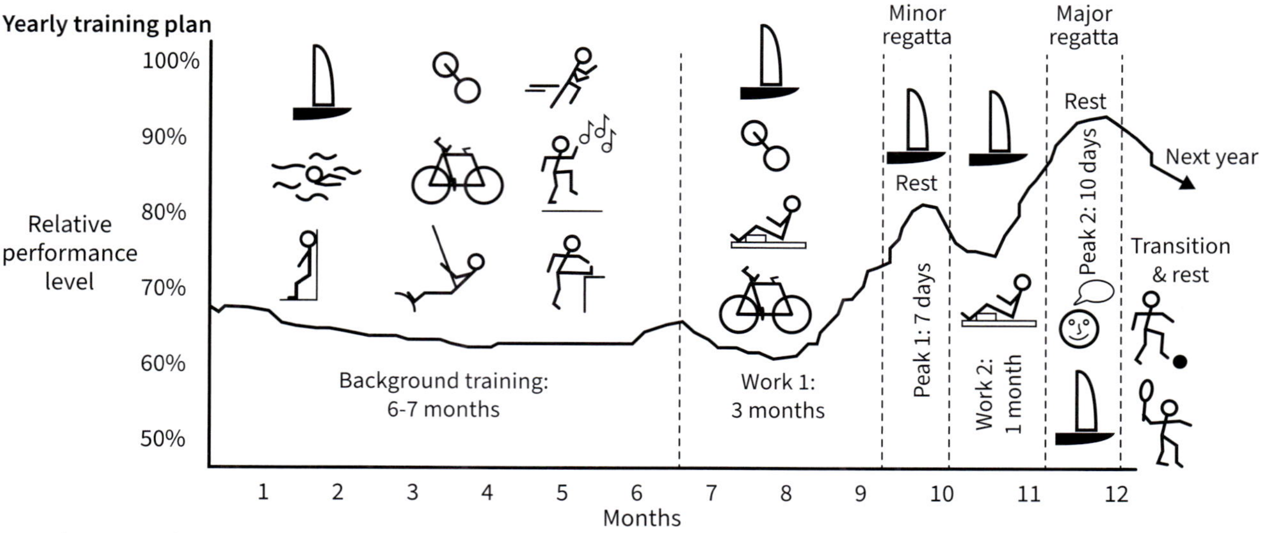

A yearly training plan, showing how training fits in with the key regattas

The yearly training chart shows a typical pattern of work, recovery and performance peaks across a season. Let's look more closely at the key phases and how each contributes to your overall performance plan.

Background Training

The background phase lays the foundation for everything that follows. It's a period of steady, progressive work that builds general fitness and prepares the body for higher loads later in the year. The goal is simple: to strengthen the body's systems – heart, lungs, muscles, joints and connective tissues – so they can handle the specific demands of hard sailing and racing.

During this time, gradually increase your overall training load. Mix sailing sessions with complementary activities such as running, cycling, swimming, gym work or circuit training. Include flexibility and mobility work too – stretching, yoga or dynamic mobility drills all help. The variety keeps motivation high while building a broad aerobic and muscular base.

Most background training should have some volume (many hours) to it but be moderate in intensity. Longer, steady efforts are the key to developing endurance and efficiency. This is also when you can safely improve movement patterns, coordination and core control – qualities that pay off when the training becomes more specific.

Think of this period as building the base of a pyramid: the broader the base, the higher the potential peak. For elite sailors, this foundation may take years to develop; for most, six to eight months of consistent, progressive work will provide a strong platform for the more intense 'Work' periods to come.

If you let your conditioning slide completely over winter, you'll spend much of the next season just trying to regain lost ground. Maintaining a modest level of fitness year-round makes every new build phase easier – and less painful – to start.

Because the main event can feel a long way off, motivation can dip in this phase. The key is to set short-term, measurable goals that feed the long-term target. For example:

- Aim to improve your 20km cycling time trial by two minutes over eight weeks
- Complete a strength programme of three gym sessions per week for six weeks
- Stretch, trigger ball and foam roll for 15 minutes after every sailing session

These small, specific goals create momentum. They give a sense of progress and keep the connection between daily training and the bigger picture alive.

Work 1

In this phase you begin converting your general fitness into sailing-specific conditioning. The focus shifts from building a broad base to training the exact movements, muscles and energy systems you rely on competing in your class.

Your sessions should now reflect the real demands of sailing – hiking, trapezing and time spent refining boat handling and decision-making under fatigue. On-the-water training becomes the backbone of your programme, supported by targeted gym, aerobic or mobility work that mirrors or complements those same patterns.

Progressively increase the overall training load by adding both volume and intensity. For example, you might build from three to six sessions a week over an eight-week block. Expect a short-term dip in freshness or performance as your body adjusts – this is part of the process. With consistency and recovery, performance will rebound to a higher level as your body adapts to the new workload.

It's during this period that fitness and technique start to merge. Use your on-the-water sessions not just to build endurance, but to sharpen efficiency – smoother movements and better timing mean more time spent making the boat quicker, and less time fighting the boat.

Peak 1

This phase marks your first mini-peak of the season – a chance to race hard and test your form without the pressure of your main event. After a solid training block, you briefly ease back to freshen up and convert training gains into race-ready performance.

The taper here is short, typically two to five days. Reduce overall training volume but keep the intensity high to stay sharp and maintain the rhythm of racing. You're aiming to feel fresh and responsive, not rested to the point of losing edge.

Choose a smaller or lead-up regatta about one to two months before your major event. Treat it as full race conditions – compete seriously, manage nerves and rehearse your routines – but know that it's primarily a checkpoint for your preparation. Use the event to gauge how your body responds to the shorter taper and to fine-tune your approach for the main peak later in the season.

These small tapers provide feedback on how much recovery you need to perform well, helping you fine-tune the balance before the main event.

How will you prepare for your next big regatta? (ILCA Worlds 2025)

How To Taper Well & Peak For Competition

The core of any good taper is simple – reduce the volume of training while maintaining its intensity.

This balance allows fatigue to fade while preserving, and often enhancing, the fitness you've built. The result is a fresher, sharper version of the same athlete, ready to perform at a higher level.

A taper isn't time off; it's a controlled reduction in workload. Sessions become shorter and less frequent, but their quality remains high.

You still push hard in parts of your training – just for less total time. This approach keeps your coordination, power and race skills intact, while giving your body time to recover and adapt.

The length of the taper depends on the demands of the event and your training history:

- For a small local regatta, one or two lighter days may be enough
- For a major regatta, start easing back three to seven days before the regatta
- Highly physical venues may warrant up to ten days, while long endurance sports such as rowing or swimming can extend that to two weeks or more

During the taper, expect to feel a mix of energy and restlessness – that's normal. You may even feel flat for a day or two as your body shifts from heavy loading to recovery. Resist the temptation to squeeze in one more session. The fitness gains from any hard work in the final few days are minimal, but the fatigue can linger into racing.

Use the taper period to polish race-specific skills. Short, sharp sessions on starts, boatspeed and handling are good, but aim to race against as many boats as you can in the same format as your upcoming regatta – that's the best and most realistic preparation. Aim to finish each session feeling switched on, not drained.

A well-timed taper does more than restore energy. It helps coordination, focus and confidence return as the body and mind align for performance. Arriving at the start line feeling fresh, alert and fully recovered is one of the clearest signs that your taper has done its job.

Scientific research shows that once a solid fitness base is built, you can maintain it for several weeks doing roughly half the training volume it took to achieve it. That means it's almost always better to be slightly under-trained but fresh than over-trained and flat.

In the final month before a major competition, the balance between intensity and volume becomes critical. The focus should shift toward high-quality, race-specific work while progressively reducing overall hours.

Training Plan – Four Weeks To Go

As the plan illustrates, intensity takes priority in these final weeks. Shorter, sharper sessions – particularly those involving racing or simulated race work – prepare the body and mind for the demands of competition while ensuring full recovery by the final week.

Weeks to go	Weekly Training Emphasis	Intensity	Volume
4	Recovery & low-intensity, medium volume training (longer sailing sessions & aerobic exercise)	Low – Medium	Medium
3	High intensity, low volume training (shorter, intense races)	High	Low
2	Lead-up competition or competition-specific training	High	Medium – Low
1	Limited competition-specific training & rest	Medium – High	Low
0	Sail well!		

Training Plan — Seven Days To Go

In the last week, quality matters most. Each day should have a clear purpose, whether that's a short burst of race practice, a technical focus or rest. Note how volume steadily drops while intensity remains high in the key on-the-water sessions.

Days to go	Activity	Intensity %	Volume (hr:min)
7	Racing – last day of warm-up regatta	100	3:00
6	Recovery day – light swim & stretch	10	0:45
5	Cycle / weights	80	1:00
4	Sail – solid upwinds / strategy	85	2:00
3	Sail – speed & starts – quality work	50-100	1:45
2	Sail – 3 good races of 20 minutes	90-100	1:30
1	Rest & light activity / stretch	10	0:30
0	First race	100 (if windy!)	

One challenge with tapering is that nature doesn't always cooperate. A storm, long calm or delayed start can throw timing off. I once arrived at a pre-Olympic regatta perfectly tapered – only for a hurricane to cancel the first two days. When racing finally started, I felt fantastic but had already missed some advantage.

Be flexible. Keep an eye on the forecast and adjust the taper if conditions look likely to delay racing.

Remember that tapering focuses mainly on the physical side of preparation, but success depends on more than fitness alone. Use the final days to check and polish everything else – your boat set-up, gear and mental routines. If it's a new venue, spend some time on the water to get a feel for the local conditions. A short, focused session in the actual race area can be more valuable than another gym workout.

Day to day, stay responsive to the weather. If a good breeze appears, go sailing; if it's glassy calm, rest or do light mobility instead. Flexibility within the plan is the key to arriving on the start line both prepared and confident.

Work 2

With your first regatta complete and the benefits of a structured taper now clear, it's time to push into the next training phase. Work 2 consolidates everything you've built so far – the base, the specific fitness and the confidence gained from racing – and uses it to lift performance another step.

Training in this phase becomes highly specific. On-the-water sessions dominate, and every session should connect directly to racing performance. Use what you learnt in the lead-up regatta to identify weaknesses and design sessions that target them. If you struggled with heavy-air hiking, mark-rounding execution or handling under fatigue, now's the time to address those gaps systematically.

Increase intensity while slightly reducing overall volume. Replace long, steady sessions with shorter, more demanding ones that mirror race conditions – repeated short races, close-quarter drills or pressure-based scenarios with other boats. Quality now matters more than quantity.

Whenever possible, train against strong local competition. The higher the standard around you, the faster your learning curve. These practice races help fine-tune boat handling, race rhythm and tactical awareness while maintaining physical sharpness.

This period is also a good time to refine your race-day processes: pre-start routines, timing and recovery between races. The aim is to enter the final taper period already operating at a high, repeatable level – confident, conditioned and ready to peak when it counts most.

End-of-year training plan

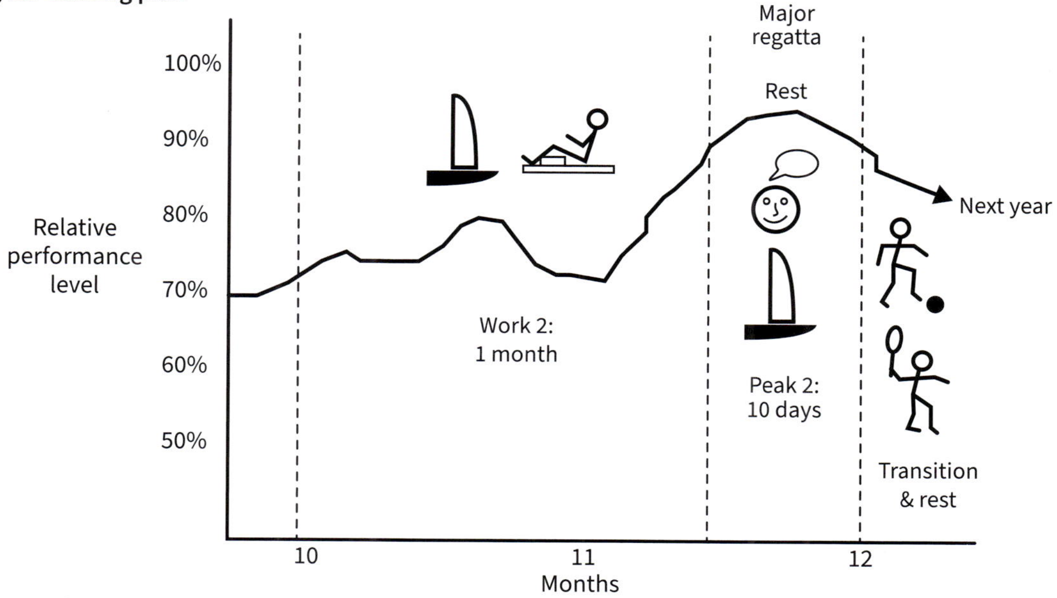

This is key to making everything come together for the final event

Peak 2

This is the point where everything comes together – the final taper and the lead-in to your major regatta of the season. After months of structured work, your goal now is to arrive fresh, confident and ready to perform at your absolute best.

As with your earlier mini-peak, the key principle remains the same: reduce volume, keep intensity high. The difference this time is in scale and precision. You're tapering for your biggest event, so the process may begin a little earlier – often 7-10 days out – with recovery, focused hit-outs and mental readiness all carefully balanced.

Use the first part of the taper to let fatigue fade while maintaining rhythm through shorter, high-quality sessions. These can include races, start reps and speed work. As the event draws closer, drop the total volume further but keep bursts of intensity so that the body stays switched on, the reflexes stay quick and coordination stays crisp.

Where possible, include multiple lead-up races within the taper period. These provide valuable decision making and technique practice under race pressure while giving feedback on readiness.

Equally important at this stage is mental preparation. Use some of the freed-up time to visualise race scenarios, re-read the race documents, review the venue, refine your routines and check all equipment thoroughly. The focus shifts from building to executing – calm confidence replacing effort and grind.

When the taper is well-timed, you'll feel lighter, clearer and faster in the boat. At this point, your job is simple: trust the work, stay fresh and let your preparation do the talking.

Transition Phase

After your main regatta, it's time to reset. The transition phase allows both body and mind to recover from months of focused work and the stress of competition. It's a deliberate step back – not complete rest, but a period of active recovery and variety that sets up the next training cycle.

Take a break from structured sailing for around four weeks. Let the body heal, re-energise and re-balance. At the same time, stay active with different sports and activities – play football, go for rides, swim, surf, wing, climb or try something new. The aim is to stay moving without the physical or mental strain of high-performance training.

This phase is also a time to reflect and recalibrate. Review what worked in your season plan and what didn't, note areas for technical or physical improvement, and think about the next set of goals. Short debriefs with your coach or training partners can be invaluable in shaping the next cycle.

By keeping active while easing away from intense training, you'll begin the next build phase from a higher baseline of fitness and motivation. Over successive seasons, these transition periods help lift your long-term performance year by year – each peak sitting slightly higher than the last.

Matilda Nicholls takes time off the water

Rolling Weekly Loading

The principles of periodisation apply on a smaller scale too. Each week or ten-day cycle should include natural rises and falls in workload – hard days balanced with lighter or rest days to let the body adapt.

Aim for two or three hard sessions a week, separated by moderate or easy days. This rhythm allows high-quality effort without accumulating fatigue.

Recovery isn't wasted time; it's when improvements occur. Too many hard days in a row only dull performance, while timely recovery keeps progress steady and reduces the risk of illness or injury.

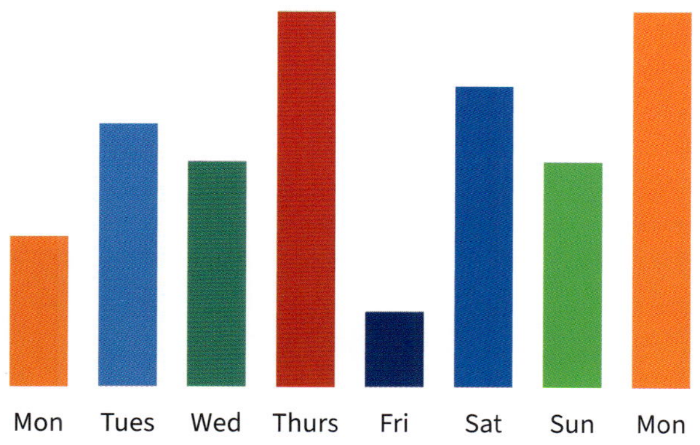

Vary the load throughout your training periods

Long-Term Planning

Over time, consistent planning and structured work add up. Each season builds on the last, provided you recover well and keep learning from experience. The aim isn't to reinvent your programme each year but to refine it – adjusting loads, timing and priorities based on what's been proven to work for you.

As skill and experience grow, the balance between training volume and quality also shifts. Elite performers often need less total training to stay sharp because years of deliberate practice have already hard-wired the essential movements, skills and decision patterns. Their challenge is fine-tuning execution and arriving at key events mentally fresh and physically primed – not grinding through extra hours.

By contrast, developing sailors still building mastery need higher training volumes to strengthen those same foundations. Repetition remains their most effective teacher. They should expect to spend more time on the water and in the gym to consolidate the technical and physical skills that experienced athletes can now maintain with less.

Whatever the level, the principle stays the same: planned, consistent work balanced with smart recovery and regular reflection. Over successive seasons, this rhythm lifts your performance baseline – each peak sitting a little higher than the last. The next step is learning how to recover better, more often, so that progress continues.

Relative training load for an Olympic cycle (out of 10)

Recovery: Revive & Survive

A single bout of very hard exercise – such as a long, windy race – can temporarily suppress the immune system, particularly in the first few hours afterwards. During this window, the body is more vulnerable to infection, so steer clear of anyone coughing or sneezing. Even a short cold or stomach bug can disrupt training or competition. Recovering well reduces this risk and supports consistent performance.

The immune system has two main roles during recovery: protecting against infection and repairing tissues stressed by exercise. Training too hard, too often or returning too soon after illness can delay full recovery and increase the risk of fatigue or sickness. A well-planned recovery routine helps avoid these setbacks and keeps progress steady.

Why Recovery Matters

Recovery begins the moment you stop exercising. How effectively you recover determines how soon you can train hard again and how much you gain from the work you've done.

In elite programmes, recovery isn't an optional extra – it's a core part of training.

Top athletes use short, purposeful recovery methods between demanding sessions – light aerobic work, mobility drills, cold-water immersion, massage or simply rest and refuelling. The quicker you restore energy, repair tissues and settle the nervous system, the better your next session can be.

Practical Recovery Priorities

After a tough day on the water – especially in heat, wind or waves – focus on these three essentials:

1. **Refuel:** Eat a balanced meal or snack containing carbohydrates and protein within 30-60 minutes of finishing to replenish glycogen and support muscle repair
2. **Rehydrate:** Replace fluids and electrolytes lost through sweat using water, milk or electrolyte drinks
3. **Restore movement:** Gentle stretching, mobility work or light activity improves circulation and reduces stiffness

Recovery Methods

Cold & Contrast Water Therapy

Cold-water immersion (10-15°C for 5-10 minutes) can reduce inflammation, soreness and perceived fatigue, particularly after consecutive race days. Alternating warm and cold immersion may help circulation, though cold alone is usually enough. Stop if you feel numb or light-headed and avoid using cold therapy less than an hour before exercise.

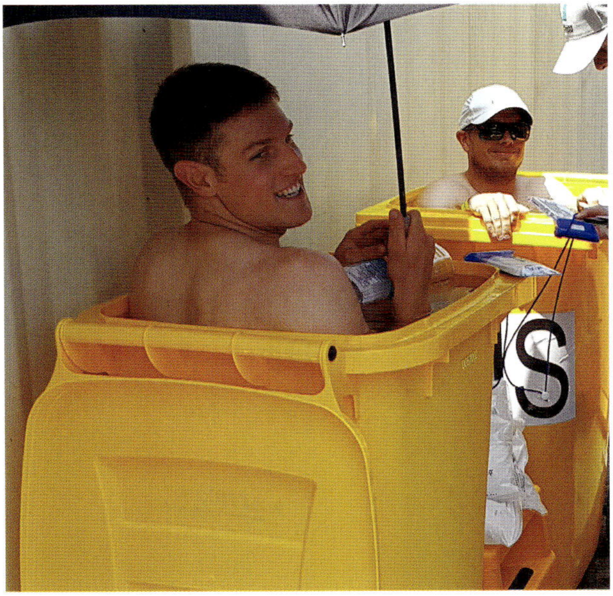

Matt Wearn and Tom Burton having ice baths

Heat & Sauna Use

Warm showers, spas and saunas promote relaxation and circulation. Used sparingly, heat exposure after training may also help cardiovascular adaptation. Avoid dehydration and excessive exposure.

Compression & Circulation Aids

Compression garments and pneumatic boots (e.g. 2XU, Skins, Normatec) can enhance venous return and reduce swelling after long travel or hard sessions. Their effects vary, but they're safe and can improve comfort and recovery readiness. The best times to use them include during long flights or drives, immediately after training or racing (and overnight if comfortable) and between regatta days to reduce leg fatigue

Sleep & Relaxation

Sleep is still the best recovery tool available. Aim for 8-9+ hours per night during heavy training and add short naps if racing early or travelling. To improve sleep quality: reduce screen time before bed, darken the room and keep a regular routine.

Good recovery sleep isn't only about hours – it's also about helping the body switch from 'fight or flight' to 'rest and digest'. Simple relaxation methods such as slow nasal breathing, progressive muscle relaxation or guided meditation can help activate the parasympathetic nervous system and improve sleep depth. Some sailors find short mindfulness or breathing sessions (3-5 minutes) before bed effective for lowering heart rate and calming pre-race tension.

Travelling sailors face extra sleep challenges. Beds, pillows and room environments change constantly – sometimes noisier, hotter or less comfortable than at home. Small strategies can make a big difference. If you can, bring your own pillow to keep some continuity and comfort. Earplugs and an eye mask are excellent for managing noisy or bright rooms, especially in shared accommodation or early-sunrise locations. Maintaining a short 'wind-down routine' – stretching, reading or breathing exercises – helps signal the body that it's time to switch off, no matter where you're sleeping.

Active Recovery & Mobility

Low-intensity activity after racing – short walk, swimming or cycling – enhances circulation and accelerates recovery without strain. Include simple mobility drills for hips, shoulders and upper back.

Sailing Recovery Routine

Phase	Key Practices	Timing / Notes
Cool-down	Drink (water or electrolyte mix)	During sail-in or immediately ashore
	Light movement, stretch hips, shoulders, back	While packing up / within 15 mins
	Eat snack with carbs + protein	Within 30 mins post-session
Post-session	Shower or cool water immersion (3-5 mins)	Within 30-60 mins of finishing
	Massage or compression garments	After shower or during travel
	Rehydrate (water or milk)	Continue for 1-2 hours post-session
Evening	Balanced meal (carbs, protein, veg)	Within 1 hour of racing
	Relaxation or breathing routine, music, light mobility	10-20 mins before bed
	Sleep (consistent schedule)	8+ hours, aim for quality

Monitoring Recovery

Track recovery with both data from a wearable as well as simply how you feel.

- Resting heart rate (RHR) and heart-rate variability (HRV) can help gauge readiness. If RHR rises by 5+ beats above normal, or HRV trends lower for several days, ease off or rest
- Keep a simple training log to rate daily sessions for intensity, fatigue and mood. Consistent patterns – such as several low-energy days in a row – are early signs that recovery needs attention

Smarter Rest

When a full rest day comes, don't just switch off completely. Use it to train other aspects of performance – mental rehearsal, strategy simulations or visualisation. Even ten minutes of imagery can help reinforce race routines.

Mental recovery is recognised as a key factor in sustaining performance. Sailing demands constant attention, decision-making and emotional regulation – all of which tax the brain. Techniques such as guided breathing, body scanning, journalling or brief mindfulness sessions can help reset focus and reduce cognitive load. Short walks in nature, music or social downtime also help the nervous system unwind.

Low-key movement, time outdoors and social recovery also play a part. Think of recovery not as doing nothing, but as preparing the body and mind to perform again.

Summary: Recover Better, Sail Better

Recovery is where adaptation happens. Balancing effort with effective rest keeps you healthy, consistent and race-ready through long regattas and training blocks. The best sailors recover deliberately – refuelling early, hydrating well, prioritising sleep, using cooling, compression or relaxation when needed, and taking care of the mind as much as the muscles.

Recovery is holistic – body, brain and mood all count. A calm, well-rested sailor is faster to learn, quicker to react and better able to sustain performance under pressure.

When Waiting For The Wind

'It is very common for sailors to be held on shore due to too little or too much wind. People would head to a café while socialising randomly or use their phones to surf around the social media posts, watch YouTube videos, play games, etc.

There's nothing wrong with all these things, but just bear in mind that anything you do is gradually 'using' and 'wearing out' your body battery.

I once experienced this after waiting ashore for a long day. When I got onto the water, after the AP (postponement) flag came down, I felt very low in energy and was not able to focus well during the following race.

I later realised that even those activities which would be considered light relaxation, like chatting, playing cards or watching movies, etc., are all slowly 'burning' our bodies' daily allowance, without being noticed.

So, after that I learnt to wait in a 'smart' way: to conserve my energy, in order to be 100% prepared and fresh once the AP came down.

What would I do? Instead of chatting and fumbling with my phone all the time while waiting ashore, I'd find some quiet places to lie down and close my eyes. Not necessarily sleeping, but just to stop using the body battery, and having a quiet time for myself.

Do keep sipping water and eat the right type of snack (not croissant or high fat and protein food) frequently in small portions in order to keep yourself hydrated and fuelled.'

(Taken from *Golden Lily – 10 Years On* by Lijia Xu – *the autobiography of ILCA olympic gold medallist Lijia Xu*)

Eight-Week Training Programme

The sample eight-week training programme below illustrates how the components of a training programme discussed in this book might fit together. While people differ in the needs and aims of their physical training and therefore there is no single ideal training programme for all people, this example roughly illustrates what a good training programme would involve on a weekly basis for someone with some background fitness. The programme could be part of the 'Work 1' period of a Yearly Plan (p57).

The programme is relatively compact and features two basic four-week periods:

- The first four weeks are for developing general fitness and so involve relatively more time cycling, swimming and weight training
- The aim of the second four weeks is to enhance specific fitness, so more time is spent sailing and this is supplemented by cycling and weight-training sessions

Throughout the eight weeks, on-the-water training makes up the bulk of the programme, from two-thirds to three-quarters of the training time per week.

Good improvements in fitness can be expected over the eight weeks, and this can be monitored by completing the Home Fitness Tests (p68) at the start and completion of the programme.

Notes On The Programme

- Before each session complete a warm-up plus stretching
- Between morning and afternoon sessions take a break of at least four hours
- Swim – wearing flippers: 100m efforts – alternate 50m kicking (lying on back) with 50m freestyle; 30 seconds rest between repetitions
- Gym – light: Follow the example for building muscle strength (p49), but complete only two sets per exercise (30-40 minutes)
- Gym – strength: Follow the strength example given earlier (p49) completely (approximately 60 minutes)
- Gym – endurance: Follow the earlier example (p50) for building muscular endurance (45-60 minutes)
- Cycle: Alternate between the cycling session examples (p51)
- Cycle / row session: As described in Seven Top Sessions (p50)
- Club race: Compete in the regular weekend races (allowing 2.5 hours)
- Regional Championships: A chance to test your fitness and skill against some greater competition. (Four races, approximately 4.5 hours sailing each day)
- Space is provided to record resting heart rate (HR) during the harder weeks and if it is found to be too high, the programme should be adjusted by substituting a rest or light activity day
- National Championships: This is the targeted regatta, so greater rest is provided in the lead-up

Sample Training Programme

Week 1:
Intensity = light | Volume = 7:15hr | 6 sessions

Mon	Rest
Tue	Gym – light
Wed	Cycle 0:45min – moderate
Thu	Gym – light
Fri	Rest
Sat	Club race
Sun	Club race

Week 2:
Intensity = medium | Volume = 10:00hr | 7 sessions

Mon	Swim – 10 x 100m
Tue	Gym – light
Wed	Sail 2hr
Thu	Gym – strength
Fri	Cycle 60min
Sat	Club race
Sun	Club race

Week 3:
Intensity = hard | Volume = 13:00hr | 9 sessions

Mon	a.m. Swim 12 x 100m | p.m. Gym – strength
Tue	Cycle 60min
Wed	a.m. Gym – strength | p.m. Sail 2.5hr
Thu	Cycle 45min (hills repeats)
Fri	Rest
Sat	a.m. massage | p.m. Club race
Sun	Club race

Week 4:
Intensity = light | Volume = 10:30hr | 7 sessions

Mon	Gym – strength
Tue	Swim 5 x 100m
Wed	Sail 2hr
Thu	Rest
Fri	Gym – strength
Sat	Club race
Sun	a.m. Cycle 60min | p.m. Club race

Week 5:
Intensity = hard | Volume = 15:45hr | 7 sessions

Mon	Gym – strength
Tue	a.m. Cycle 45min | p.m. Sail 2hr
Wed	Gym – strength
Thu	Sail 2hr
Fri	Rest
Sat	Regional Championships (2 races)
Sun	Regional Championships (2 races)

Week 6:
Intensity = medium | Volume = 13:00hr | 7 sessions

Mon	Cycle / row session
Tue	Sail 2hr
Wed	Gym – strength
Thu	Sail 3hr
Fri	Gym – endurance
Sat	Club race
Sun	Club race

Week 7:
Intensity = med-hard | Volume = 12:30hr | 8 sessions

Mon	a.m. Swim 10 x 100m | p.m. Gym – strength
Tue	Sail 2hr
Wed	Cycle 60min
Thu	a.m. massage | p.m. Sail 2hr
Fri	Gym – endurance
Sat	Club race
Sun	Club race

Week 8:
Intensity = light | Volume = 9hr | 6 sessions

Mon	Gym – endurance
Tue	Sail 2hr
Wed	Gym – endurance
Thu	Sail 2hr
Fri	Rest
Sat	Club race
Sun	Cycle – light

Week 9:
National Championships

Mon	Rest
Tue	Races 1 & 2
Wed	Races 3 & 4
Thu	Races 5 & 6
Fri	Races 7 & 8
Sat	Races 9 & 10
Sun	Rest

Home Fitness Test

It's often difficult to judge exactly how fit you are for sailing – you may be strong in some areas but weak in others. In this chapter are some fitness tests you can use to more accurately judge your fitness for sailing. All the equipment you need is a set of weighing scales, a floor, a tape measure or ruler, a table, some form of aerobic exercise and, for hiking sailors, a hiking bench.

These tests can be completed at regular intervals, for example every three months, so you can plot your progress and the change in fitness following training. Complete each test carefully, using a similar technique during a subsequent re-test to avoid false results. Also, following a warm-up, always complete the tests in the order listed so that any effects of fatigue from one test to the next are consistent.

You can download a test sheet to record your performances over time. Click on the QR code or go to www.fernhurstbooks.com, search for 'Fitness to Win' and click on 'Additional resources'.

Body Weight

Measure your weight on an accurate set of scales while wearing minimal clothing and at a consistent time of day, for example, after waking up and going to the bathroom but before breakfast.

Flexibility: Sit & Reach And Shoulder Mobility Tests

Sit & Reach Test

Sit on the floor with the legs straight in front, no shoes, toes pointing up. Place one hand over the top of the other, fingertips overlapping and elbows straight. Then, lean forward as far as possible, sliding your hands towards or past your toes.

The legs should remain straight and full stretch must be held for three seconds to avoid bouncing. The distance the fingers are from the soles of the feet is measured with a ruler (if the toes cannot be reached a negative score is recorded).

Flexibility Targets	
Club sailor	+6cm
National level	+12cm
International level	+18cm

What The Test Measures: A general flexibility test that is also a practical test of the ability to lean in to adjust sail controls while hiking.

Sit & Reach Test: Sitting on the floor with the legs straight, measure how far you can reach relative to your toes

Shoulder Mobility Test

Stand tall and reach one arm over the shoulder and down your back while reaching the other arm up from below to try to touch the fingers together behind you. Measure the overlap (positive score) or gap (negative score) between the fingertips. Record both sides, as sailors often have one shoulder looser than the other.

What The Test Measures: Shoulder and upper-back flexibility are vital for effective sheeting, reaching across the boat and maintaining good posture when hiking or trapezing.

Shoulder Mobility Test: Reach one arm over your shoulder and the other arm from below and measure the gap / overlap between your hands – do both sides

Mobility Targets

Club sailor	Fingers almost touch
National level	2cm overlap
International level	5cm+ overlap

What If You Score Low On These Tests?

If you're not as supple as you could be, your ability to move smoothly around the boat and reach into awkward positions is limited. During growth phases, bones can lengthen faster than muscles, temporarily reducing flexibility. While females are generally more flexible than males, both should work consistently to maintain good range of motion. The best gains come from regular stretching and / or joint strength and mobility work immediately after training, when the muscles are warm.

Core Endurance Tests

Abdominal Curl Test

Lie on the floor with knees bent at 90° and feet flat. Rest your hands on your thighs and slowly curl up until your fingertips touch the bottom of your kneecaps, then lower back down. Move smoothly – about one curl every three seconds – and stop when form breaks down (jerky movements, feet lifting or not reaching the target).

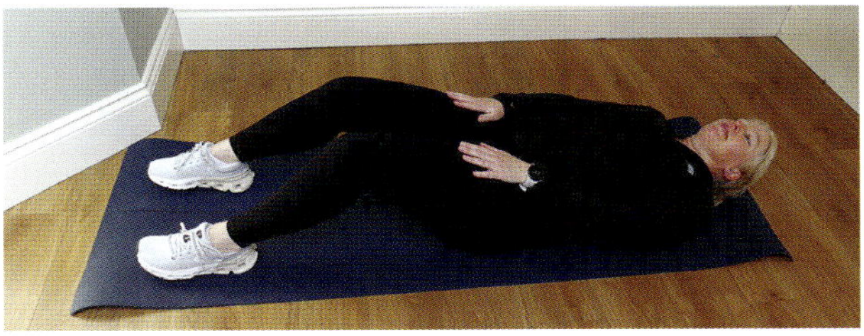

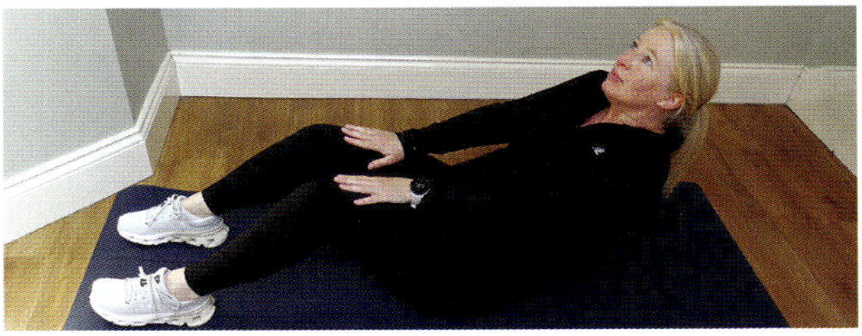

Abdominal Curl Test: From lying of the floor with knees bent, slowly curl up until your fingertips touch the bottom of your kneecaps, then lower back down

Abdominal Endurance Targets

Club sailor	20 reps
National level	50 reps
International level	80+ reps

What The Test Measures: This test focuses mainly on the trunk flexor muscles, which move and stabilise the trunk during hiking, pumping and other dynamic movements on the boat.

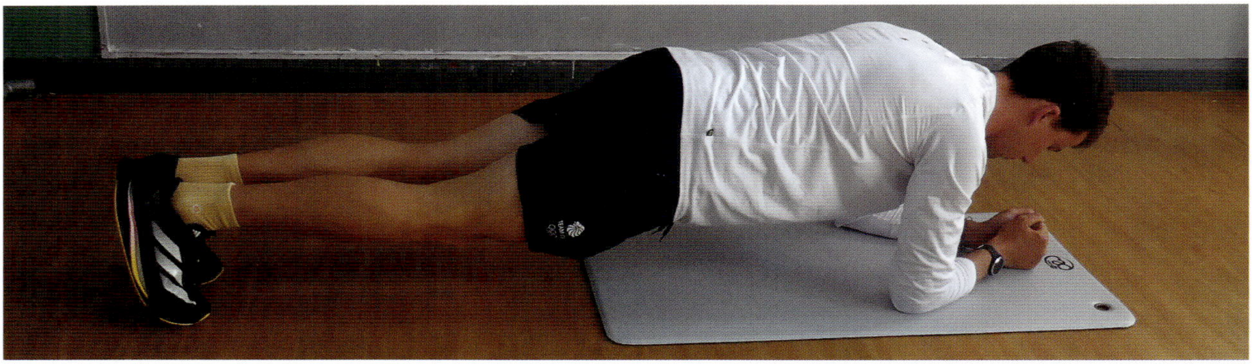

Plank Hold Test: Forearm plank position – hold for as long as possible

Plank Hold Test (A17)

Adopt a forearm plank position with elbows under shoulders, body straight and core engaged. Hold the position for as long as possible without sagging or lifting the hips.

Plank Endurance Targets	
Club sailor	60sec
National level	3min
International level	4-5min

What The Test Measures: The plank assesses overall core endurance – abdominals, lower back, hips and shoulders – providing a fuller picture of trunk stability and control.

What If You Score Low On These Tests?
Weak core endurance makes it harder to hike, trapeze or pump for extended periods and can increase strain on your lower back. Include regular core work in your programme – short, consistent sessions two or three times a week make a big difference.

Body Weight Pull-Up (*Horizontal Row*) Test (E5)

Lie under a bar or edge of a table and rest your feet on the floor. With hands roughly shoulder width apart, pull your chest up to touch the bar or table and lower. Maintain strict form: your knees should remain bent at about 90 degrees; resist using your legs to help push; make sure your repetitions are full.

Body Weight Pull-Up Targets	
Club sailor	10 reps
National level	20 reps
International level	30+ reps

What The Test Measures: This tests the strength of the arm and back muscles and can indicate your sheeting or pumping ability.

Body Weight Pull-Up Test: Lie under a bar or table edge and pull your chest to touch the bar or table

What If You Score Low On This Test?
Muscle strength is best improved by doing weight training or similar exercises. Turn back to Seven Favourite Training Sessions (p46) for examples of these. Developing greater strength in your upper body will make sheeting the sails and adjusting the sail controls easier.

Hike-O-Matic Test

You might recall back in the Seven Top Sessions chapter (p46) I mentioned the Hike-o-Matic. That same set-up will be used here.

To prepare the bench, mark identical reference points under each side so you can align the dowel in the same position each time. Label the positions clearly (for example, 1 = easy, up to 5 = hard hike). Use a small file or saw to make shallow notches to help the half-inch dowel settle neatly into place.

Set up your hiking bench with reference points to align the dowel

With the dowel under the bench, sit and hike as usual. When your centre of gravity moves outboard of the dowel, the bench will tip slightly backward. The goal is to determine how long you can hold that position before fatigue forces you to sit up. You can test at any position (1-5), depending on your height and hiking strength.

Start by setting the dowel so the test lasts roughly between 1 and 15 minutes. It will take some trial and error to find the right level. Allow a couple of brief 'forward tips' during the test if needed but return immediately to the hiking position.

For extra realism, wear your hiking pants and attach a mainsheet simulator (a rope and short length of shock cord) to replicate sheeting load. Use a stopwatch or phone timer to record time to fatigue, and, if possible, video the test to compare body angle and technique at each re-test.

Hiking Targets

It's difficult to set universal targets for the Hike-O-Matic because bench design and construction vary, which can change the load significantly. For that reason, the test works best as a self-reference: set it up the same way each time, record your time, and aim to improve on your own result over time rather than comparing to fixed benchmarks.

What The Test Measures: A very functional measure of hiking endurance – your ability to hold static muscle contractions in the thighs, hip flexors, lower legs and core.

Optional Simplified Version – Wall-Sit Test

If you don't have access to a hiking bench, you can use a Wall-Sit Test as a substitute. Stand with your back flat against a wall, knees bent at 90 degrees, feet shoulder-width apart and hold for as long as possible.

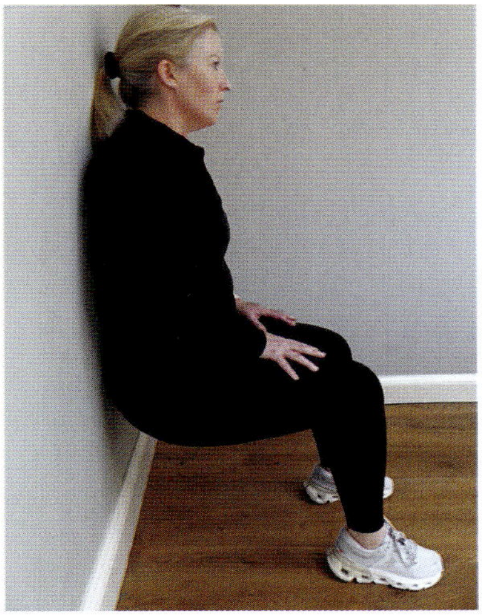

Wall-Sit Test

Wall-Sit Test Targets

As with the Hike-O-Matic, it's difficult to set exact targets for the wall-sit, as small differences in foot position or contact with the wall and floor can affect the difficulty. As a rough guide, aim for well over a minute, but use the test primarily as a self-check: keep the set-up consistent, record your time, and track your own progress over time rather than chasing a fixed benchmark.

What If You Score Low On This Test?

More hiking-like training may be needed. Remember that the static muscle activity in hiking makes it quite different from most other forms of exercise, so the more specific training you do the better. This test can really hurt! But your endurance can be increased by occasionally swapping the load from one leg to the other to encourage blood flow through the muscles.

Aerobic Test: Personal Time Trial

There's no single piece of equipment required for this test – it's up to you. What matters is that you choose a mode of exercise you can repeat under similar conditions each time.

You can run, swim, cycle or use an indoor exercise bike. The idea is simple: set yourself a fixed distance or time and complete it as fast as you can. The test should last between 5 and 30 minutes so it reflects real racing endurance rather than sprint ability.

Examples:

- Run: Record the time to complete 3km, 5km or 10km
- Swim: Record time for a 1km or 1500m swim
- Indoor Bike
  - Either record your average power (watts) over a 10-minute maximal effort
  - Or record the time to ride 5 or 10km at your best pace

If you have a heart rate monitor or smart watch, note your average and maximum heart rate during the test. These data give a useful measure of how efficiently your aerobic system is working.

What The Test Measures: Your aerobic capacity – the ability to sustain moderate-to-high intensity effort for an extended period. For sailors, it reflects the fitness needed for long racing days and repeated upwind efforts.

What If You Fail To Improve?
If your performance plateaus, it might mean you're already very fit, or that your training needs more volume, intensity or variation. Try mixing in intervals (e.g. 3 × 8 minutes at threshold with 2min rest) or longer steady sessions to raise your endurance ceiling.

What exercise you choose for the personal time trial is up to you

Fitness For Young Sailors

When you're between nine and seventeen, school, friends and other sports can easily compete for time on the water. That's normal – sailing development in these years should stay fun and exploratory, not rigid or specialised. Young sailors learn movement patterns quickly, and this is the ideal window to build balance, coordination and efficient body control rather than fitness for its own sake.

Early Skill Learning

Children learn most effectively when taught efficient movements rather than left to endless trial and error. Core skills such as tacking, gybing and mark roundings are best practised in controlled environments – flat water, moderate breeze, minimal pressure. Quality coaching here pays off for life: the sailor acquires clean mechanics before bad habits form.

Multi-Sport Advantage

Early specialisation in a sport might look like a shortcut to success, but research shows it's usually not. Kids who focus on one sport too soon often drop out later as peers overtake them physically or mentally. A young sailor who also plays other sports – cycling, gymnastics, football – builds the coordination, agility and resilience that later translate directly into better sailing.

Physical Development Through Adolescence

Approx. Age	Key Changes – Girls	Key Changes – Boys	Coaching & Training Focus
9–11yrs (pre-puberty)	Rapid coordination gains; similar strength to boys	Steady growth; same strength as girls	Emphasise fun, games, balance & variety
12–14yrs (puberty on-set)	Growth spurt, flexibility may drop; strength still limited	First muscle & height surge; awkward movement phase	Teach posture, stretching, light core work
15–17yrs (post-puberty)	Near-adult size, endurance improves	Large gains in muscle & aerobic capacity	Begin structured strength & conditioning with supervision

After puberty, boys usually develop greater upper-body strength, while girls maintain higher natural flexibility. Both sexes benefit from mobility work – especially hamstrings and hip flexors – to offset time spent hiking.

Parents and coaches should match sailor size and power-to-weight with rig and boat choice, so competition stays enjoyable and safe.

Practical Training Guidelines

For young sailors, the goal isn't to 'train hard' but to move often and move well. The best programme is usually simple and fits naturally around school and sailing.

On days off the water, a bit of light cycling, swimming or even a jog with friends is enough to build endurance.

These are also the years to develop posture and flexibility – learning to stretch after sailing or adding ***short plank*** (A17) and ***Copenhagen plank*** (H5) holds, can make a huge difference later when the loads increase.

Flexibility work should focus on the hips and hamstrings, since these are the areas that tighten most from time in small boats and sitting at school desks. Short, regular stretching sessions are far better than the occasional long one.

When it comes to strength, body-weight movements such as ***push-ups*** (C1), ***squats*** (D3) and ***step-ups*** (D4) are the safest place to start.

Once a sailor reaches around sixteen and has stopped growing quickly, they can begin more formal resistance work under supervision – focusing on good technique, not on how heavy the weights are.

Above all, training for youth sailors should be consistent, not extreme. Two or three short land-based sessions a week, in addition to regular sailing and active play, are usually enough to set them up for long-term success.

Case Studies

To show how these principles work in real life, the following case studies highlight four young sailors at different stages of development. Each example illustrates how training can fit naturally into a busy week, balancing sailing with school, sport and recovery. Details of the exercises mentioned here are in the Appendix.

Case Study 1: Ella (12yrs, Optimist)

Subject:

Height:	1.48m
Weight:	42kg
Sailing:	3yrs
Goals:	Improve coordination, learn race routines, have fun
Sails:	2 days per week + school PE + netball training

Typical week:
2 days sailing, 3 days school PE or team sport, 1-2 light flexibility sessions after sailing, plus plenty of unstructured outdoor play.

Ella is energetic and fearless in breeze but loses concentration during long waits. Her programme blends short, focused sailing sessions with agility games and swimming. Strength training is minimal; the emphasis is movement quality and agility. She often uses balance discs or a hiking simulator for a few minutes after sailing to build posture awareness.

Case Study 2: Luke (13yrs, Optimist → ILCA 4)

Subject:

Height:	1.65m
Weight:	54kg
Sailing:	5yrs
Goals:	Maintain technique through growth, build endurance
Sails:	2 times per week plus school sport and skate-boarding

Typical week:
2 days sailing, 2 short youth-strength circuits, 3-4 sessions of skateboarding or school sport, 2 flexibility sessions.

Luke is midway through a growth spurt and sometimes feels 'all arms and legs'. His coordination comes and goes from week to week, but his attitude stays positive. He keeps flexibility sessions short and frequent, using dynamic stretches before sailing. On land he performs a 20-minute youth strength (body weight) circuit twice a week (e.g. ***prone alternate arm and leg*** (B1), ***sit-up to stand*** (A1), ***push-ups*** (C1), ***body weight pull-ups*** (E5), ***back extension*** (F1)). His coach emphasises smoothness over speed and checks hiking technique regularly to prevent postural strain.

Luke enjoys mixing skateboarding and sailing because both require balance and quick reactions. As his strength builds, he's encouraged to focus on control rather than power. Over the next year, his challenge will be to stay patient through the awkward stages of growth while continuing to enjoy the sport.

Case Study 3: Sarah (16yrs, ILCA 6)

Subject:

Height:	1.66m
Weight:	62kg
Sailing:	4yrs
Sailing History:	Started in Optimist, now ILCA 6
Goals:	Develop fitness and increase body weight for ILCA 6; compete in ILCA 6 Youth Worlds and World Sailing Youth Worlds
Sails:	2-3 days per week – Club races, regional regattas, nationals; extra sessions in holidays

Typical week:

3 days sailing, 5 days light cycling (commute to school), 2 days beginner strength sessions (body-weight only), 1 rest day.

Sarah has nearly completed her growth spurt. She avoids heavy lifting, relying on body-weight strength circuits (***push-ups*** (C1), ***assisted chin-ups*** (E2), ***squats*** (D3), ***planks*** (A17)). Daily cycling builds her aerobic base. Flexibility work targets hamstrings and lower back – areas critical for hiking. She's starting to recognise the mental side of performance and keeps a brief training diary noting what went well each day.

Some days Sarah gets a bit tired. Her week isn't overly demanding; it's the extra activity with friends – swimming, late nights, spontaneous outings – that adds up. She's learning to balance recovery and training, knowing that rest is part of progress. Her commute to school by bicycle is an efficient way to stay fit while keeping life simple. With time and steady practice, she's building both endurance and independence that will serve her in the transition to senior competition.

Case Study 4: Josh (17yrs, ILCA 7 candidate)

Subject:

Height:	1.80m
Weight:	75kg
Sailing:	6yrs
Goals:	Prepare for senior-class transition; increase strength and recovery discipline
Sails:	4 sessions per week plus gym and cardio cross-training

Typical week:

4 days sailing, 3 supervised gym sessions (resistance circuits and rowing erg), 2 mobility / recovery sessions, 1 rest day.

On land, Josh trains under supervision three times per week, combining resistance circuits, rowing-erg intervals and hiking-bench endurance. Recovery has become as important as workload – he schedules one full rest day and uses sleep tracking to stay consistent. He and his coach plan training blocks around regattas and school exams, understanding that a tired sailor learns little on the water.

By 17, Josh's body is close to adult strength, so the focus is refining technique, mobility and smart preparation. He's learning that quality beats quantity and that small habits – proper warm-ups, good form, good nutrition, enough sleep – matter more than extra hours in the gym. His balanced approach sets him up well for the physical and mental demands of the ILCA 7.

Mental & Social Development

Everyone's motivation is a bit different. Some sailors like setting their own goals and pushing themselves in competition; others prefer being part of a close group and getting support from teammates and coaches. Both approaches work – what matters is finding what keeps you engaged and enjoying your sailing. Remember, it's okay to make mistakes. That's how you learn and improve.

Try building a few simple habits to stay on track:

- Keep a short training log: Jot down what you did and how it felt
- Note your energy, sleep and school workload – they all affect performance
- Each week, write one thing that went well and one thing you want to improve next time

These small check-ins help you notice patterns, celebrate progress and take more control of your own development – both on and off the water.

And for coaches and parents, it's about guiding this process with encouragement and patience, helping young sailors build confidence, self-awareness and a lasting love of the sport.

Summary

The takeaway for young sailors is simple: stay active, stay balanced and enjoy the process. Sailing at this age should build confidence and coordination, not pressure. Match the boat to the sailor's current size and strength so that sessions feel achievable and rewarding. Keep developing flexibility, posture and balance before worrying about heavy gym work.

Encourage a mix of sports, movement and fun on the water – that's what builds lifelong athleticism. And when tiredness creeps in, remember that recovery is part of training too. A rested, happy sailor will always learn more than an exhausted one. With these foundations in place, young sailors will be ready for the demands of senior competition – and, more importantly, they'll still love the sport when they get there.

Fitness For Masters Sailors & Old Salts

Sailing is one of the few sports that stays with you for life. It draws a community of sailors over 35 who vary widely in ability, experience and motivation – but all share that same pull to keep learning and competing.

Your level of fitness often influences the boat you choose to sail. Take the example of Santiago Lange: a multi-Olympian who, at the age of 54, returned from lung-cancer surgery to win gold in the mixed Nacra 17 class at the 2016 Rio Olympic Games alongside Cecilia Carranza Saroli. His long career, built on decades of Olympic experience across different classes, shows how skill, resilience and determination can continue to drive success well beyond youth.

That sort of achievement in today's more physical dinghy and board classes would be rare, but Masters events flourish precisely because sailing rewards both brains and brawn.

There's plenty of general advice on fitness for older athletes, but sailing has unique demands. Hiking and sheeting create long isometric efforts that can spike blood pressure. Masters sailors should build cardiovascular and muscular conditioning gradually before windy regattas, prioritising good breathing, posture and progressive loading.

How The Body Changes With Age

Peak power may be behind you, but usable strength lasts a long time if you keep training it. Regular resistance work keeps you strong where it matters most and helps protect against the usual aches and strains.

Endurance doesn't disappear either – it just needs a bit more maintenance. A mix of steady aerobic work and short bursts keeps fitness levels high without leaving you drained.

Recovery is the biggest shift with age. You probably already know how your body responds to hard days; the difference now is that recovery takes a little longer. It's not about doing less, but about pacing things so the quality stays high. Alternate demanding sessions with easier ones, give your joints time to settle, and keep gentle movement going between sails. You'll recover faster by staying mobile than by doing nothing. Above all, good sleep and steady routines make the biggest difference – they're what allow you to turn up ready again tomorrow.

Training Considerations For Masters Sailors

Start every session with a 10-15-minute warm-up that gets the hips, hamstrings, ankles, upper back and shoulders moving. The goal is to raise body temperature, loosen joints and activate muscles so you move smoothly.

Strength is important. Two whole-body sessions each week – combining leg work, pulling and pushing movements, and core bracing – will build the kind of strength that translates directly to sailing.

For aerobic work, combine steady efforts of 30-45 minutes with occasional short intervals such as six rounds of two minutes hard, two minutes easy.

Allow at least 48 hours between hard strength sessions, and use easy spins, walks, mobility work and good sleep to recover. Maintain balance and coordination through single-leg exercises, wobble-board drills and reactive movements to keep your agility alive.

When preparing for regattas with back-to-back days, consider using cold-water immersion to reduce soreness – but save it for race periods, not after every gym session during training blocks, since frequent use can limit strength gains.

Finally, if you have high blood pressure or any cardiac risk factors, get medical clearance before starting new or intense exercise routines.

These are the key ingredients of a sustainable training plan for masters sailors – practical, adaptable and built to last. As we get older, the way we stay fit changes. Some sailors focus on maintaining strength for hiking, others on joint health or recovery between races. The right balance depends on your goals, time and how your body responds.

Case Studies

The following case studies show how these principles play out in real life – three sailors at different ages and stages, each with their own approach to keeping fit, staying competitive and enjoying time on the water.

Case Study 1: Doug, The Pragmatist

Subject: 44 years old
Sailing on and off for 25 years
Sailing history: Experienced many boats and crew roles; now settled in an ILCA 7. Races at club level with occasional larger events
Goals: Enjoy sailing; be a contender for the Club Championship next season; body weight acceptable

Typical sailing: 1-2 days / week – weekend club racing, occasional after-work sails and regattas

Programme (what Doug does and why)

- Doug's approach is simple and sustainable: Enough to keep him strong without taking over his week
- **Strength** (2 × wk): One 45-min full-body gym session; one 30-min home circuit (pulley / rope, shock cord, body-weight). Includes ~10-min trunk bracing (e.g. ***Pallof Press*** (A15)) and hip / hamstring work (e.g. ***Romanian Deadlift*** (D5)) to protect the area given a history of low-back niggles
- **Stamina** (2 × wk): Commute cycle once weekly (weather-permitting); 20-min interval hiking-bench session with shock-cord-loaded mainsheet to mimic race loads
- **Mobility & recovery:** 10-15min stretching post-sailing / strength; cold-water walk after windy days. He stays flexible, swapping days or shortening sessions when life gets in the way
- **Technique:** He adds occasional non-race sailing sessions to refine skills without pressure

Weekly plan (typical)

Monday	Strength
Tuesday	Rest
Wednesday	Stamina (cycle) or Sail
Thursday	Strength
Friday	Stamina (hiking bench)
Saturday	Sail
Sunday	Rest

Progression: Add ~2 minutes per week to hiking time until ~30 minutes total; gradually increase resistance / loads in strength sessions. Keep the two rest days to support recovery.

Case Study 2: Ian, The Adjuster

Subject: 63 years old

Long dinghy background; moved to a two-person keelboat due to knee pain with hiking

Sailing history: Decades of club and regional regattas; values tactics and boat-handling efficiency

Goals: Sail pain-free, maintain crew work capacity, recover better after regattas

Typical sailing: Weekly racing plus practice when crew is available

Programme (joint-friendly fitness):

- **Endurance** (3 × wk short): Alternates 30-min brisk walks and 25-30-min rowing-machine sessions (e.g. 8 × 2min steady-hard / 2min easy)
- **Strength** (2 × wk): Slow-tempo ***step-ups*** (D4), ***split-squat*** (D3) ***holds, cable / band rows*** (E3) and shoulder external rotations; includes isometric mid-back work for posture
- **Mobility** (daily 10 min): Hips, thoracic extension / rotation, ankles
- **Recovery & work habits:** One full rest day after regatta weekends; avoids long sitting stints (uses a sit-stand desk)
- **On-the-water focus:** Emphasise efficient, economical movement patterns and avoid sudden, high-load or exaggerated efforts that are beyond comfort. Controlled, well-timed movements reduce joint strain and lower injury risk while assisting performance

Weekly plan (typical)

Monday	Mobility (10min) + Strength
Tuesday	Walk (30min) (brisk)
Wednesday	Rowing intervals (25-30min)
Thursday	Mobility (10min) + Strength
Friday	Easy walk (20-30min) or rest
Saturday	Sail (race or practice)
Sunday	Recovery day (light mobility only)

Progression: Add a set or modestly increase range of motion before adding load; keep intervals consistent but nudge total work time upward across weeks.

Case Study 3: Margaret, The Connector
Subject: 65 years old
Crews on a RS200
Sailing history: Enjoys physical teamwork and travel; past shoulder instability
Goals: Maintain grip and pulling strength; improve balance and posture; stay socially connected
Typical sailing: Weekly racing plus practice in season

Programme (posture, pull strength, balance):

- **Pilates** (2 × wk): Focus on spinal alignment, hip mobility, and shoulder control
- **Endurance** (2 × wk): 20-30min lap swimming; occasional short pool intervals
- **Strength** (2 × week, short): Simple upper- and lower-body work such as ***band rows*** (E3), ***pull-ups*** (E5), gentle ***push-ups*** (C1), ***step-ups*** (D4) and light hand-grip exercises
- **Recovery:** 15min after sailing with foam roller + light massage-gun work for shoulders; evening walk for circulation
- **Social & motivation:** Post-sail coffee with helm is 'non-negotiable' – keeps adherence high!

Weekly plan (typical)

Monday	Pilates
Tuesday	Swim (20-30 min)
Wednesday	Strength (bands + step-ups, 25-30 min)
Thursday	Mobility walk (20 min)
Friday	Strength (push / pull + grip, 25-30 min)
Saturday	Sail
Sunday	Recovery walk + light mobility

Progression: Increase rowing band tension and step-up height gradually; keep shoulders symptom-free by stopping 2-3 reps before form degrades.

Bringing It All Together

What matters most isn't how much you do, but how regularly you do it. A couple of focused sessions each week – some strength, a bit of power, steady aerobic work and mobility – will keep you strong and capable without wearing you down. Know the difference between useful effort and overdoing it and give recovery the respect it deserves. If you've got back-to-back sailing days, a cold dip or ice bath can help take the edge off.

Masters sailing rewards the things you already do well: pacing yourself, making smart decisions and using experience to stay efficient on and off the water.

Fitness For Club Sailors

Most club sailors don't have the time or interest to train like Olympians – and that's perfectly fine. Sailing once a week is one of the best escapes from a busy life, and a little fitness in between those sails can make it even better. The aim isn't to turn you into an athlete; it's to make every session on the water feel easier, smoother and more enjoyable. A few minutes of regular movement each week can reduce fatigue, make manoeuvres feel lighter and help you finish the day feeling good rather than worn out.

Even casual sailing challenges the whole body. You're constantly shifting your balance, crouching, bracing and pulling. Improving mobility and general strength helps you move around the boat more comfortably, while a basic level of endurance keeps your energy up through long days or gusty conditions. Think of it as keeping yourself in tune, just as you would with your boat – a bit of regular maintenance keeps everything working properly.

Before heading out (or even on the sail out), take five minutes to warm up. Move your shoulders and hips through their range, twist the torso side to side, roll your ankles and finish with a few light squats. These small movements loosen joints, activate key muscles and get you ready to react.

On the water, focus on efficiency. Smooth, well-timed movements use less energy and reduce the strain that comes from trying to muscle the boat around. If you catch yourself pulling or hiking with everything you've got, that's usually a cue to adjust technique rather than work harder.

Between sails, try to fit in a couple of short exercise sessions each week – even just half an hour – to keep your body moving well. Combine a few body-weight exercises such as ***squats*** (D3), ***step-ups*** (D4) and ***push-ups*** (C1) with some ***resistance-band rows*** (E3) or core holds like ***planks*** (A17) or bird-dogs. Mix that with simple aerobic activity such as brisk walking, swimming or cycling for 20-30 minutes. Add a few balance challenges like standing on one leg while brushing your teeth or using a wobble board. You don't need equipment or a gym; the goal is just to stay strong and coordinated enough that sailing feels familiar.

After sailing, take a few minutes to cool down. Walk around the boat park, stretch your hamstrings and shoulders, and have a drink of water. If you've been out in heavy weather, a short cold shower or dip can help take the edge off muscle soreness. These habits keep you comfortable the next day and ready for your next sail.

Above all, keep it realistic. You don't need to overhaul your life to feel fitter on the water. Move a little every day, keep your joints mobile and build a touch of strength and endurance. Staying active through the week will make your time on the water more enjoyable and keep you sailing well for years to come.

Even club sailors will benefit from a little fitness and mobility work

PART 5

OTHER CONSIDERATIONS

Avoiding Injury

Sailing might not be a body-contact sport, and water is usually a forgiving surface, but injuries are still common – from bruises and cuts to fatigue-related strains or long-term sun damage. Avoiding injury keeps your training on track, the racing fun and rewarding.

Some injuries are minor annoyances that slow you down; others can develop quietly and become serious if ignored. Lapses in care – staying wet for too long, skipping sunscreen, sailing through pain – add up over time.

Fatigue is often the first link in the injury chain. When you're tired, concentration slips: a mistimed duck under the boom, a missed wave, a small collision. Add cold, heat, glare or travel fatigue and it's easy to make a mistake that puts you out for weeks.

Eyes

Long days on the water can be tough on your eyes. Glare from the sea, sails and deck makes it harder to spot gusts and lulls, adds to fatigue and over time can cause serious UV damage.

The lenses in modern sunglasses are excellent – improved optics and coatings enhance contrast on the water and can reveal subtle changes in wind texture and wave shape. In certain conditions, good polarised lenses can make gust lines, lulls and reflections stand out more clearly, reducing strain and helping you read conditions faster.

There's still a trade-off, though. Even a few drops of water or salt spray on the lenses can distort vision and reduce clarity, especially when you're trying to see fine ripples or small shifts in pressure. How practical sunglasses are depends on the day – in light-air or flat-water racing they're usually fine, while in rougher or 'splashier' conditions they can be more trouble than they're worth. It's a personal choice, and one option is to wear them up to the start and again after racing, which helps keep the eyes fresher overall.

Beyond performance, sunglasses and hats remain the best defence against long-term UV exposure. Chronic glare and UV reflection can lead to eye irritation and, over time, pterygium – a cloudy growth on the surface of the eye that can slowly spread across the pupil and affect vision. It's common among sailors and surfers who spend long hours exposed to wind and sunlight.

Surgery can remove a pterygium, but recurrence is possible, so prevention is key. A peaked hat, wrap-around sunglasses that block 100% of UV-A and UV-B rays and limiting unnecessary exposure outside of racing times will all help protect your eyes and reduce fatigue.

Limit exposure to UV rays to protect your eyes

Skin & Sun

Sailors everywhere spend long hours exposed to sun, wind and reflected glare from the water – a combination that's hard on the skin and, over time, can lead to premature ageing and an increased risk of skin cancer. The message is the same no matter where you sail: protect your skin before extended time in the sun.

In countries like Australia, where UV levels are among the highest in the world, rates of skin cancer are also the highest. Health authorities around the world recommend avoiding suntanning and instead following a simple routine of protection. In Australia it's often summarised as 'Slip, Slop, Slap, Seek and Slide' – slip on protective clothing, slop on sunscreen, slap on a hat, seek shade and slide on sunglasses.

For sailors, hats and clothing should always be the first line of defence. Choose lightweight, breathable, long-sleeved tops and neck buffs made from UV-protective fabrics.

Sunscreen comes next – apply it to exposed skin when dry, at least 20 minutes before heading out, and reapply every two hours or after getting wet. Look for a broad-spectrum SPF 50+ (or at least SPF 30+) product that's water-resistant for four hours.

Because we're often on the water longer than expected, many sailors carry a small stick or tube of sunscreen in their buoyancy aid (PFD) to reapply between races. Zinc-based creams are excellent for high-exposure areas like the nose, ears and lips since they don't wash off easily, though they shouldn't be used over large areas because they can block sweat and interfere with the body's natural cooling.

Cuts, Scrapes & Foreign Bodies

Watch for sharp edges on fastenings and fittings – exposed bolts, screws or corners can cause small cuts that may become infected if not cleaned properly. Keep fittings smooth and well maintained to avoid these hazards.

If you do get a cut or abrasion:

1. Rinse thoroughly with clean (fresh) water
2. Apply antiseptic (povidone-iodine or chlorhexidine) for several minutes
3. Use a waterproof dressing if you must sail again before it heals – clear polyurethane film dressings work well. You may need to protect the dressing with some extra tape to keep it intact on the water
4. Remove once dry, unless more exposure risks re-opening it

Watch for redness, swelling or persistent pain – signs of infection. Avoid sailing barefoot and wear well-fitted booties or trainers to protect against barnacles and fittings.

Good nutrition and hydration support faster healing; vitamin C, zinc and protein are particularly important when training heavily.

You're going to spend a lot of time exposed to the sun, wind and reflected glare from the water – protect your skin accordingly

Common Boat-Related Injuries

Most sailing injuries happen when it's windy. Everything accelerates – tacks, gybes, recoveries – and small timing errors can cause big impacts. The vang (kicking strap) is tighter, the boom sits lower and you're working harder and faster.

To reduce risk:

- Warm up before sailing: 5 minutes of dynamic movement improves agility
- Keep your workspace tidy: Control tails, cleats and lines that can snag a foot or hand
- When tired, double your awareness around the boom, mainsheet blocks and traveller
- Treat bumps or strains early with ice for 10-15 minutes, rest and gentle stretching once swelling settles

Marine stings, ear infections, blisters and splinters are common too. Most can be prevented with protective gear, regular cleaning and avoiding polluted water.

Fitness & Injury Prevention

Strong, conditioned muscles and joints are your best protection. Fatigue and poor posture account for many sailing injuries – especially lower-back and shoulder pain.

As already indicated earlier in the book, a good programme includes:

- Aerobic base work (cycling, running, swimming) to delay fatigue
- Strength training for hips, core, shoulders and legs
- Mobility and recovery sessions to maintain range of motion
- Sport-specific hiking or trapeze drills to condition key positions

Strong fitness allows you to recover faster from knocks and handle multiple races per day without breakdown. But the lesson isn't to push through every pain – it's to listen to your body and sense the difference between effort and warning signs.

Overuse injuries (especially shoulder impingement and lumbar strain) are increasingly common in active sailors. Periodised strength and flexibility work, plus tips from physio and coach (where available), helps manage them early.

Summary

Avoiding injury isn't about wrapping yourself in bubble wrap — it's about consistency:

- Protect your skin and eyes every day
- Keep the boat tidy and maintained
- Build strength and mobility year-round
- Treat niggles early and rest when your body asks for it

A healthy, uninjured sailor trains more, learns faster and ultimately sails better.

There is a greater potential for injury on windy days

Lower Backs: The Stayed Back

Back pain is common in small boat sailors, especially with long periods of hiking or pumping. The spine behaves like a flexible mast: the vertebrae transfer force between upper and lower limbs, while muscles, tendons and ligaments act like stays to brace and position it. Because this 'rig' is heavily loaded, the lower back cops a lot of stress.

Many sailing positions and habits influence how the low back feels. Twisting the trunk to look to the other side of the course, holding awkward positions under load or sailing through fatigue can trigger spasms or aggravate sore tissues. Pain might ease once you're warm and moving, but recurring pain can affect your range of motion, decision speed and confidence. The good news: most non-specific low back pain responds well to sensible loading, technique tweaks and consistent, simple exercises.

Lower-back issues often stem from:

1. Local deconditioning
2. Imbalances around the hips and trunk
3. Task stress from hiking / trapezing / pumping and unsupported sitting

Causes vary – so if pain persists, see a professional to rule out specific pathology. What follows are general principles that help most sailors.

Hiking Muscles

When hiking, the hip flexors and quadriceps support the torso in its outboard position, while the abdominals, obliques and deep trunk muscles brace to prevent excessive arching of the lower back – essentially acting as your backstay system. The challenge increases when those trunk and lateral muscles are under-trained, fatigued or when you push the leg – trunk angle too far (for example beyond ~150° of hip extension). Motivation to 'send it' can lead to over-hiking, causing increased lumbar arch, elevated compression and shear loads.

Maintain a neutral spine – your ribcage and pelvis should stay aligned, so the lower back isn't heavily arched or rounded. Let the hips and thighs provide the power while the core holds you steady. This typically gives you a strong righting moment and moderates tissue stress – your 'performance + durability' sweet spot (more on this in the next section). Because hiking isn't strictly static, your body will need to make frequent micro-adjustments – small resets of the pelvis, ribcage or foot-strap – to maintain form through long beats or variable conditions.

A strong core isn't just about doing endless sit-ups – what matters in hiking is the ability to hold a stable, braced posture under load. The trunk has to transfer force between the legs and upper body for long periods, with the occasional controlled flex. Both stability and flexion work are useful, but stability-based exercises are probably a little more important overall, since they build the endurance and postural control that best match the demands of hiking.

Also don't forget your 'side-stays': the obliques and lateral hip / trunk musculature. These often get overlooked, yet they're critical for resisting trunk rotation and side-bend when you're hiking while sheeting, steering or trimming. Train them with side planks, loaded carries, controlled rotations.

Strength, endurance and technique all matter. Research shows that sailors with higher quadriceps strength and better trunk-flexor endurance sustain hiking longer with lower perceived effort and lower risk of spinal stress.

So, in your training and on the water:

- Emphasise trunk and lateral core endurance rather than only leg-hiking capacity
- Use hiking-specific drills (hiking benches, gym ball extensions) to train the hip-trunk interplay and reactive micro-adjustments
- Monitor your form especially when fatigue sets in – the risk of lumbar arch and bracing failure increases as quads and core tire
- Prioritise hip / trunk strength and endurance early in the season, so you're ready for a higher volume of sailing later in the competition period

Hiking Health vs Performance

There's a trade-off between hiking health and hiking performance.

The goal is to find a position that delivers maximum righting moment without putting unnecessary strain on the lower back.

The photos show a range of common hiking positions, each rated out of five for health (lower = higher risk of back injury) and performance (higher = greater righting moment). Add the two together (the higher the score the better) to find the best compromise.

Health = 1 Performance = 1 Total = 2

1. Excessive rounding of back; weight too far inboard

Health = 1 Performance = 2 Total = 3

2. Twisting the trunk like this can be ok for a moment, but holding this position places damaging loads on the lower back

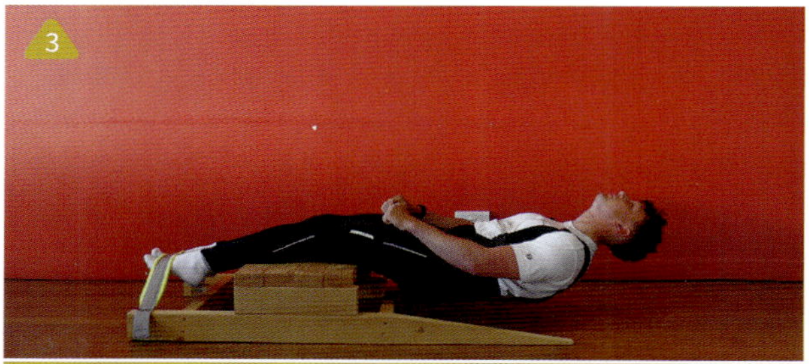

Health = 1 Performance = 4 Total = 5

3. This looks like a big effort but the body is too low to the water for top performance and there is a massive load via the hip flexors on the lower back

Health = 4 Performance = 3 Total = 7

4. This is a nice hiking position – good for moderate winds

Health = 4 Performance = 3 Total = 7

5. A nice, neutral spine position but could be a little more 'up and out' – see next

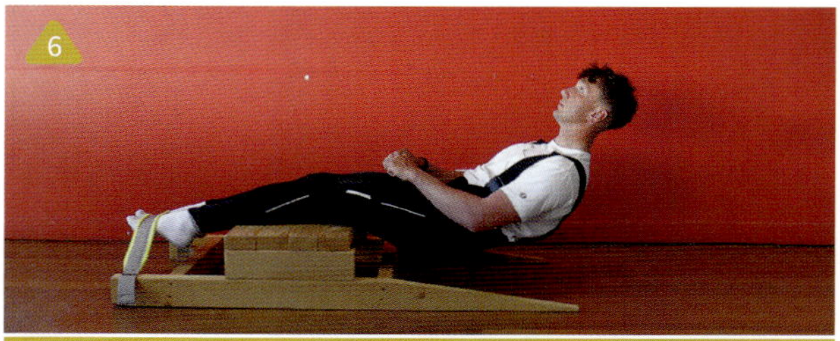

Health = 5 Performance = 5 Total = 10

6. Lower back is in a nice, natural position, shoulders are neutral too and a high righting moment is also being produced. This requires strong core muscles to maintain

As the examples show, the most effective posture combines a neutral spine – one that's neither rounded nor over-arched – with strong leg involvement. This alignment reduces load on the lower back while still generating solid righting moment. In simple terms, you're aiming for a position that feels powerful yet sustainable across a long beat.

Excessive rounding or twisting can increase the risk of muscle strain or joint irritation, particularly if held for long periods. Over-arching the back also drives compression through the lumbar spine and hip flexors. Instead, aim to keep the trunk long and braced, the hips and thighs doing the heavy work, and the shoulders relaxed.

A good test is whether you can make small posture adjustments without losing boat trim – those micro-corrections indicate good strength / endurance through the core and hips. In moderate conditions, the best positions usually feel 'up and out' rather than 'flat and strained'.

Preventing Back Pain

Lower-back pain is common among sailors, often linked to long periods of hiking or working in positions that shorten and tighten the hip flexors. When these muscles are under tension, they restrict hip extension and increase shear and compressive forces on the lumbar spine. To reduce strain, it's important to strengthen the core while maintaining mobility and length through the hips.

When hiking, the hip flexors are active for extended periods and rarely stretched. Over time this can tilt the pelvis forward, exaggerate the lower-back curve and load the spine unevenly. After sailing or hiking practice, make a habit of opening the hip joint – moving the thigh back under the body – to restore normal hip extension and reduce lumbar stress.

Open up the hip joint after sailing or hiking practice

Not all back pain has the same cause. Contributing factors can include muscle imbalances, leg-length differences, weak core or gluteals and leaning too far back when hiking. The most effective approach depends on which of these factors apply to you.

Aside from the usual must-dos – like bending your knees rather than your back when lifting boats – the following exercises help maintain spine mobility, stability, and muscular balance.

Simple Mobility & Rehabilitation

These exercises help restore motion, reduce stiffness and encourage balanced spinal movement:

- **Pelvic tilt:** Lie on your back with knees bent, feet flat. Gently draw your lower abdomen in to flatten the small of your back against the floor. Hold 5-10 seconds
- **Knee-to-chest:** Lie on your back, pull one knee toward your chest or shoulder and hold 5-10 seconds. Repeat on the other side

1. Knee-to-Chest: Lie on your back

2. Pull one knee toward your chest or shoulder and hold 5-10 seconds

- **Cat-camel:** On hands and knees, round your spine upward (cat), then slowly drop your belly and lift your chest (camel). Move smoothly through the range 8-10 times

1. Cat-Camel: On hands and knees, round your spine upward (cat)

2. Then slowly drop your belly and lift your chest (camel)

- **Child's pose stretch:** From hands and knees, sit back on your heels and reach your arms forward, lengthening the spine. Hold for 15-30 seconds
- **Prone lumbar extension:** Lie face down, prop up on your elbows or press part-way up on your hands, keeping hips on the floor. Hold briefly, then relax. Repeat five times

Child's pose stretch: From hands and knees, sit back on your heels and reach your arms forward, lengthening the spine

Strength & Stability

These exercises improve the endurance and coordination of the deep stabilising muscles (transversus abdominis, multifidus, obliques) that protect the spine during hiking and boat handling.

Gym ball

- ***Seated single-leg balance*** (B2)
- ***Prone alternate arm and leg lift*** (B1)
- ***Gym ball prone single-leg off*** (B5)

Core exercises

- ***Forearm plank*** (A17) (and ***Copenhagen plank*** (H5) variations)
- ***Dead bug*** (H3)
- ***Pallof press*** (A15)
- ***Back extension hold*** (F1)

Include these at the beginning, middle or end of your gym or conditioning sessions to maintain a strong, balanced core that supports posture and reduces spinal load both on and off the water. Focus on control and endurance – frequent, low-load stability work and anti-rotation exercises are more protective and transferable to sailing than occasional high-intensity efforts.

Travelling On Aeroplanes

At some point in your sailing journey, you'll probably travel to a big event – maybe a regional, national or even world championship – to see how you measure up against a wider fleet. Travelling for competition is a great way to learn more about preparation, recovery and performing in new environments. Getting the travel side right – managing jet lag, time zone changes and recovery – can make a real difference to how quickly you find your rhythm and perform at your best when it matters most.

Jet Lag

Crossing time zones disrupts the body's circadian rhythm, affecting sleep, digestion and alertness. The more zones crossed, the greater the disruption – though smart management can cut recovery down to 3-4 days.

Before flying:

- From a day or two before you fly, shift sleep and mealtimes 1-2 hours toward your destination (earlier for eastward, later for westward)
- Get morning light before eastward trips, evening light before westward ones
- Stay active but avoid heavy training within 24 hours of departure

In flight:

- Set your watch to the destination time and try to behave as if already on that time
- Rest if it's night there; stay awake and move if it's day
- Drink water regularly, avoid alcohol and eat in line with destination mealtimes

After arrival:

- Get sunlight early in the day to reset your clock
- Generally avoid naps, but if you must, set an alarm for under 30 minutes and match your normal bedtime
- Do light activity (walk, spin, stretch), but delay hard training for 24-48 hours
- Melatonin may help sleep onset when timed correctly

Jet Stress

Even without changing time zones, long-haul travel exposes you to jet stress – a combination of low cabin humidity, reduced air pressure, restricted movement and noise. These can lead to dehydration, fatigue and muscle stiffness.

To reduce jet stress:

- Drink around 250mL of water or electrolyte drinks per hour of flight
- Limit alcohol and caffeine
- Use earplugs and an eye mask to reduce sensory fatigue
- Perform in-seat stretches and walk around the cabin every 1-2 hours to reduce risk of deep vein thrombosis (DVT)
- Compression socks may further reduce leg swelling and improve venous return
- Use a saline nasal spray or damp face cloth to prevent drying of the nose and throat, which can reduce the risk of respiratory infections
- Sugar-free chewing gum or lozenges can help maintain saliva flow and oral defences
- At stopovers, raise your legs above heart level for a few minutes to help drain fluid and restore circulation

Look to reduce the effects of flying

Adapting To Different Climates

If your destination is much hotter or colder than home, allow at least 3-5 days of acclimatisation before heavy training or racing.

If you're travelling somewhere hot, you can help your body adjust beforehand. Spending time in a sauna, doing Bikram-style yoga, wearing extra layers during light training or even taking hot baths in the week before departure can mimic heat exposure and improve tolerance once you arrive. In hot environments, monitor hydration by checking urine colour (aim for pale yellow) and body weight to ensure fluid balance.

In cold climates, the focus shifts to retaining heat and protecting against chill. Layer your clothing smartly: use moisture-wicking base layers, insulating mid-layers and a windproof outer layer. Avoid cotton, which traps moisture. Extend your warm-up to raise body temperature before training or launching, and keep extremities warm with thermal socks, gloves and a beanie. Stay well-fuelled – your body burns more energy to stay warm – and remember to hydrate regularly, as cold air can still dehydrate you through breathing. After training, change promptly into dry clothing, have something warm to drink and restore warmth gradually.

Managing temperature changes well not only keeps you comfortable but also helps maintain a strong immune system – especially important when travelling, where new environments can increase your risk of getting sick.

Avoiding Sickness

Staying healthy while travelling can be just as important as tuning your equipment. New environments, busy schedules and long journeys can all make you more vulnerable to illness, so focus on the basics that keep your body resilient:

- Wash or sanitise hands frequently, especially before meals
- Stick to freshly cooked food and safe water sources
- Avoid sharing drink bottles, utensils or towels
- Use insect repellent in mosquito-prone areas
- Maintain good sleep, hydration and balanced meals – your immune system depends on them

Prepare for the temperature of your destination

Lifestyle Factors

Regular training should lead to steady gains in your sailing fitness and skill. Yet even a well-planned programme can be quietly undermined by small lifestyle factors. These issues are easy to overlook because their impact builds slowly – but over time they can erode recovery, focus and performance.

Your body functions as a system. Every input – from sleep and nutrition to environment and stress – affects how efficiently that system operates.

Addressing the small things isn't glamorous, but it often determines whether you reach your full potential or plateau too early.

Hidden Drains On Performance

I once worked with a sailor who felt flat and unmotivated despite sticking to a well-structured training routine. After months of frustration, a simple blood test showed low iron levels – an easy fix that completely changed her energy and focus.

It was a reminder that even small, unseen factors can quietly hold you back.

Your environment can have the same effect. Poor bedding, disrupted sleep or stale air all make recovery harder than it needs to be.

A supportive mattress, a cool, dark room and a short wind-down routine that limits screens before bed can all improve sleep quality and mood.

These small adjustments don't seem dramatic, but over time they add up to real, consistent gains.

Structuring Life Around Training

Time is one of the most valuable performance resources. Olympic campaigns stretch over four years or more, so how you design your life around training matters as much as what you do on the water.

Minimising daily travel, arranging flexible work or study commitments, and living close to your training base all free up hours for rest, analysis and recovery. With today's options for remote work and hybrid study, athletes have more control than ever over how they use their time – use that flexibility wisely.

Matching Body Type To Boat Class

Your physique should align with your chosen boat (see p14). A sailor who is 175cm (5 foot 9 inches) and struggles to maintain 82kg may find the ILCA 7 too demanding in heavy air but could excel crewing on a 470 where lighter weight is an advantage.

Choosing a class that fits your natural build isn't a compromise – it's a strategic decision. The closer your body is to the optimal profile for the boat, the more effectively you can train, recover and perform.

Managing Long-Term Aches & Pains

Many chronic issues – tight hips, sore backs, stiff necks – aren't caused by training itself but by what happens outside it. Sitting at a desk all day reinforces poor posture and restricts mobility essential for hiking and trimming.

Alternating between sitting and standing, using an active chair or gym ball or standing desk and taking short movement breaks each hour helps maintain spinal health and pelvic mobility. These simple habits build body awareness that directly transfers to your sailing posture and endurance.

Building Resources & Support Networks

Progress depends on the quality of your environment. Financial resources and equipment are part of that, but so are coaching, mentorship and training partners. A strong training partner provides competition, accountability and feedback – things technology can't replace.

Your resources should also include digital tools: GPS tracking, onboard data, video analysis and wearables provide feedback beyond what the eye can see. Used intelligently, they help you identify trends, refine technique and manage fatigue before it becomes a problem.

Motivation & Enjoyment

The sailors who stay at the top for years usually share one trait: they love the sport itself. They're driven by curiosity and the pursuit of mastery, not by rankings or fear of failure.

When motivation is internal – a genuine love of the challenge – it creates resilience and openness to learning. When it's external – based on results, comparisons or others' approval – it tends to fade under pressure.

The best way to sustain motivation is to enjoy the process. Reflect after each race, notice what you learnt and celebrate the small steps forward. Long-term success grows from consistent engagement, not constant judgment.

Takeaway

It's easy to focus only on the hours you spend training, but the rest of your life counts just as much. The way you sleep, recover and manage your time all feed into performance on the water. Get those things working for you, and training stops feeling like a grind and it starts to work for you.

Enjoying your sailing has an important role in your improvement

'Like Riding A Bike': Sailing Skills

Sailing is made up of countless small, specific skills. Every movement you make to trim, steer, balance or hike is a skill in itself. But these aren't always easy to learn or refine – and it's this challenge that often limits how well we sail.

Once a skill is properly learnt, something remarkable happens: a relatively permanent change occurs in both your brain and body. The skill starts to feel familiar, automatic, even effortless – just like riding a bike. The body learns not only what to do but how much, how fast and when. The goal of training, then, is to help the body and mind learn and retain these movement patterns as efficiently as possible.

Building Skills That Stick

Sailing demands a huge range of coordinated movements – steering upwind, balancing through waves, gybing in breeze, trimming through lulls. To keep improving, we need to help the brain encode these skills so they can be recalled automatically under pressure.

Once a skill is deeply learnt, it stays with you. I learnt that after twenty years away from skiing. From the age of eight to 18, I was lucky to spend at least a few days each winter on the snow, and by the end of that period I was pretty capable on the slopes. Then, from 18 to 38, my focus and money went entirely into sailing. When I finally got back on skis, I was nervous that all that skill might have vanished. But after a few gentle runs, it returned almost immediately. It reminded me that time spent mastering the basics with accuracy is never wasted – those patterns stay stored, ready to be reactivated even decades later.

How We Learn Movement

Modern motor learning research shows that we don't just store fixed movements; we develop adaptable schemas – flexible blueprints that let us apply the same skill in different conditions. The more varied our practice, the more robust those schemas become.

For example, practising roll tacks in flat water, chop and waves strengthens your ability to adjust automatically. Repetition matters, but repetition with variation – what researchers call contextual interference – leads to skills that hold up better in unpredictable, real-world racing.

Focus & Cues

When a skill becomes familiar, it's easy for attention to drift just when precision is needed. Simple cue words can bring focus back to key elements of the movement.

For tacking a boat, the classic cue word sequence of 'Roll, Dash, Hike, Trim' works beautifully:

- **Roll:** Feel the boat's balance as it turns into the wind
- **Dash:** Cross smoothly and efficiently
- **Hike:** Stabilise the boat and accelerate
- **Trim:** Fine-tune sails and balance out of the tack

Research shows that cues are most effective when they direct focus externally – toward the boat or the result – rather than internally on the body. Thinking 'flatten the boat' works better than 'extend your legs'.

Breaking Down & Building Up

When learning a complex skill, it often helps to isolate sections of the movement. You might practise just the exit of a tack or the roll timing. Once that part feels natural, integrate it back into the full sequence. The aim is always transfer – combining the parts into one smooth, fluid movement that holds up in competition.

Practice Design

'Practice makes perfect' is too simplistic. It's more accurate to say practice makes permanent – and perfect practice makes progress. Repeating a movement incorrectly just reinforces errors.

Deliberate practice means working with intention:

setting goals, seeking feedback and making small adjustments each time. Short, focused sessions that stretch your limits are more effective than long, easy ones. Varying conditions and challenges make the skill more adaptable.

Think of it like cutting grooves into a record. Each repetition deepens the groove, but variety ensures you can adapt the rhythm when conditions change. Good sailors carve strong grooves – but also learn how to remix them on demand.

Becoming Highly Skilled

You can tell when a sailor has achieved a high level of automaticity. In pressure moments, the expert appears calm, unhurried and efficient. Movements blend smoothly and adapt naturally to gusts, waves and traffic. The novice, by contrast, looks rushed and inconsistent – sometimes producing a great manoeuvre, but unable to repeat it.

Experts combine consistency with flexibility. They can execute precisely yet adjust instinctively to new situations. Their focus isn't on their body but on the boat's behaviour and the outcome. That's the essence of expert performance – fluidity without conscious control.

Similar But Conflicting Skills

Skills that look similar can sometimes interfere with one another. Tennis and squash, for example, both use racquets, yet the swing patterns and timing are different enough that one can disrupt the other.

The same principle applies to sailing. Every boat has its own 'feel' when it comes to steering and balance. Switching classes takes time as your internal model recalibrates. Allow that adaptation period before judging performance and avoid switching too close to a major championship in your primary class.

Summary

Skills that last aren't built by mindless repetition, but by purposeful, varied practice. Each time you train with focus, your brain strengthens the pathways that control movement and learns how to adjust those skills for different conditions. The mix of repetition and variation helps the body and mind remember what to do automatically, even when the pressure is on. In the end, good basics don't fade – they just sit quietly in the background, ready when you need them.

FINALLY

The exercises and ideas in this book are not just for seriously competitive sailors. You may sail mostly in local competitions and go to a bigger regatta once a year to see where you're at; you'll be better than last year if you're fitter and can handle the boat well. The reassurance you get from sailing better will, I hope, help you achieve whatever your goals may be.

Get out on the water as much as you can and have some great sailing!

All skill – light wind requires delicate sail trim and boat balance

APPENDIX

GYM EXERCISES

How To Use This Section

The following sailing-useful exercises are designed to build general strength – the foundation for control, power and injury resistance in sailing. Strong legs, trunk and shoulders support longer hiking efforts, smoother transitions and better handling of sheet loads and body movement under pressure.

The recommended sets and repetitions reflect a general strength focus: loads that feel challenging but still allow good range of motion and sound technique throughout each set. As a guide:

- 3-4 sets of 6-10 repetitions for major strength exercises (e.g. squats, presses, pulls)
- 2-4 sets of 10-20 repetitions for smaller or stability-focused movements (e.g. core, rotation or shoulder control)

Not all of these exercises need to be performed in one session – and they shouldn't be. A typical workout might include six to eight exercises in total, selecting one or two from each major area: legs, upper body and core.

Think in terms of a week of training rather than a single day. For example, one session might focus on legs and trunk stability (for hiking strength), while another targets pulling and rotation (for roll tacks and sheeting control).

You'll also see many of these exercises mentioned elsewhere in the book – in sections on hiking, trapezing, periodisation and injury prevention. At the start of each exercise, we've indicated the pages of the book the exercise is mentioned so you can refer back to those for guidance on how each exercise fits within a full training session or a particular phase of your programme.

Above all, aim for consistency and control: quality movement and posture come before added load or extra volume.

For each group I have recorded a video to introduce the exercises and demonstrated some of them. Scan the QR code at the start of each section to watch the video.

A. Core / Abdominal Exercises

Scan to watch video

A.1. Sit-Up

(See p42, 75)

Purpose: Develops strength through the front of the trunk and hip flexors. A very functional exercise for dinghy sailors as it builds general core endurance and control for hiking and movement in the boat.

Equipment: None.

Recommended Training: 3 sets of 10-15 repetitions. Move smoothly, avoiding momentum or arm swing.

How To Do It: Lie on the floor with knees bent and hands lightly behind the head or touching the forehead. Raise the trunk to almost vertical, performing full sit-ups smoothly. Avoid jerking or pulling on the neck. Speed: 1 second up, momentary pause at the top, 1 second down.

Variations:

Twisting Sit-Up: As you rise, twist to bring one elbow toward the opposite knee. Twist alternate sides each repetition to engage the obliques.

Sit-Up To Stand: From a full sit-up, continue the motion to roll forward and stand up powerfully and smoothly. Builds coordination and power through the core and hips – similar to moving across the boat in a tack. Speed: 2 seconds up; momentary pause standing; 2 seconds down.

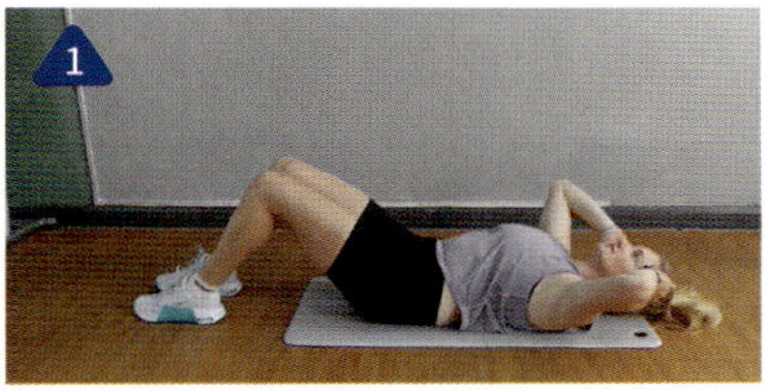

1. Lie on the floor with knees bent and hands lightly behind the head

2. Raise the trunk to perform full sit-ups smoothly

Variation: Twisting Sit-Up

A.2. Crunch

(See p46, 47)

Purpose: Focuses the effort on the upper abdominals with less hip flexor involvement than full sit-ups.

Equipment: None.

Recommended Training: 3-4 sets of 10-20 repetitions. Shorter range of motion, controlled tempo.

How To Do It: Lie on the floor with knees bent and hands lightly behind the head or touching the forehead. Lift the shoulders and upper back slightly off the floor, keeping the lower back in contact with the ground. Avoid pulling the neck forward. Speed: 1 second up; no hold; 1 second down.

Variation: Twisting Crunch: Twist the trunk so the right elbow moves toward the left knee, alternating sides.

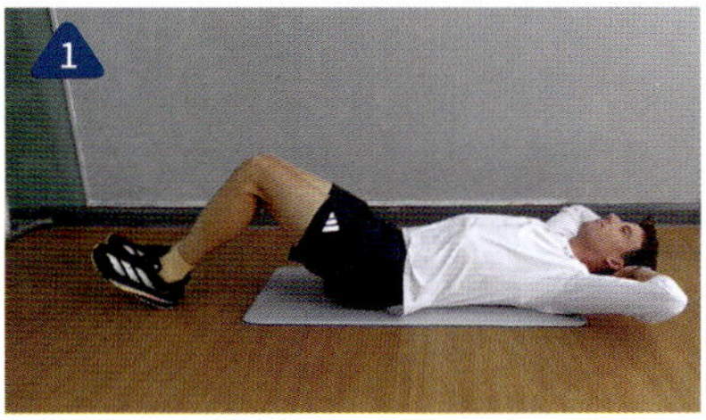

1. Lie on the floor with knees bent and hands lightly behind the head

2. Lift your shoulders and upper back slightly off the floor, keeping the lower back in contact with the ground

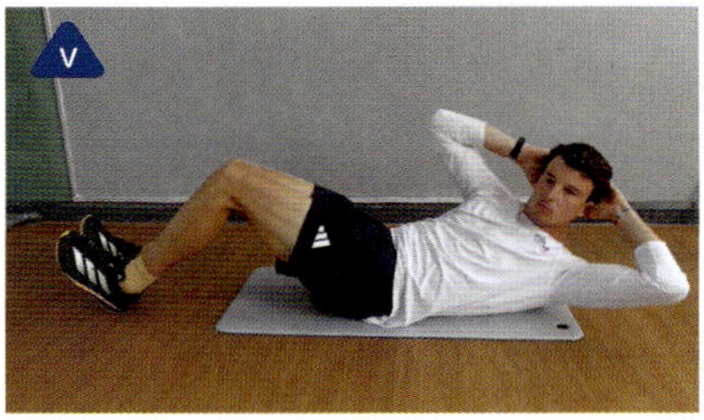

Variation: Twisting Crunch

A.3. Side Raise (Elevated)

Purpose: Strengthens the obliques and deep lateral trunk muscles, improving side stability and power when hiking.
Equipment: Gym ball or back-extension machine.
Recommended Training: 2-3 sets of 10 repetitions per side.
How To Do It: With your feet anchored, lie on a gym ball or back-extension machine, with the trunk parallel to the floor and one hip pointing down and your hands lightly behind the head or touching the forehead. Lower and lift your torso through the side muscles, keeping the shoulders aligned with hips. Speed: 1 second up; no hold; 1 second down.

1. With your feet anchored, lie on a gym ball with the trunk parallel to the floor and one hip pointing down and your hands lightly behind the head

2. Lower and lift your torso through the side muscles, keeping the shoulders aligned with hips

These core / abdominal exercises will increase your ability to hike

A.4. Hiking Sit-Up

Purpose: Mimics the hiking posture while training the core and hip flexor muscles under similar joint angles to those used in sailing.

Equipment: Gym ball, back-extension machine or hiking bench.

Recommended Training: 3 sets of 10-15 repetitions.

How To Do It: On a back-extension bench or gym ball, position yourself as if hiking with your feet anchored and your arms crossed on your chest. Lower and lift your torso, no lower than trunk horizontal to the floor. Avoid arching backwards. Speed: 2 seconds down; no hold; 1 second up.

1. On a gym ball, position yourself as if hiking with your feet anchored and your arms crossed on your chest

2. Lower and lift your torso, no lower than trunk horizontal to the floor

Variation: Hiking Throw Down: Sit in a hiking position on a hiking bench, back-extension apparatus or gym ball. Lift the trunk upward using the hiking muscles (similar to a sit-up). As the trunk rises, a partner (standing behind you) meets the movement with their hands on the shoulders and applies a short, brief, controlled push back down or slightly to one side. Absorb the push down, then immediately drive back up again, into your partner's hands. The training partner should vary the height from which the shoulders are thrown down. Speed: Start this at a slower pace for a few reps while you both get the hang of it, then speed up to 1 second up and 1 second down pace.

1. On a gym ball, position yourself as if hiking with your feet anchored and your arms crossed on your chest

2. Lift the trunk upwards using the hiking muscles

3. Your partner applies a short, brief, controlled push back down which you absorb, then drive back up again into your partner's hands

A.5. Hiking Medicine Ball Throw

Purpose: Builds dynamic trunk power and coordination while holding a hiking position.

Equipment: Gym ball, back-extension machine or hiking bench and medicine ball.

Recommended Training: 2-3 sets of 8-12 throws per side using a 2-5kg ball (start light).

How To Do It: On a back-extension bench or gym ball, position yourself as if hiking with your feet anchored, holding a medicine ball. Throw the medicine ball up in the air using one or both hands, catching it as it returns. Vary throw height and direction (double handed or from one hand to the other). A hard exercise when a heavier ball is used.

1. On a back-extension bench or gym ball, position yourself as if hiking with your feet anchored, holding a medicine ball

2. Throw the medicine ball up in the air using one or both hands

3. Catching it as it returns

1. On a back-extension bench or gym ball, position yourself as if hiking with your feet anchored, holding a medicine ball

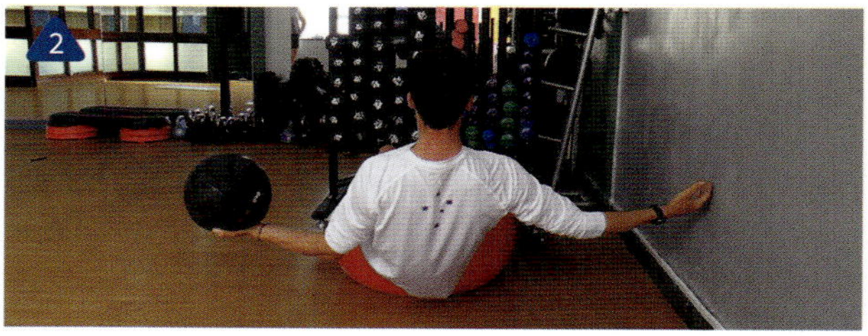

2. Throw the medicine ball up in the air from one hand to the other

A.6. Toe Touch

Purpose: Strengthens the obliques and lower abdominals through rotation and control.

Equipment: None.

Recommended Training: 3 sets of 12-16 touches each side.

How To Do It: Lie on your back with knees bent. Curl the torso up slightly (shoulders off the ground) and then alternately touch each ankle. Speed: One ankle touch per second, or a little quicker.

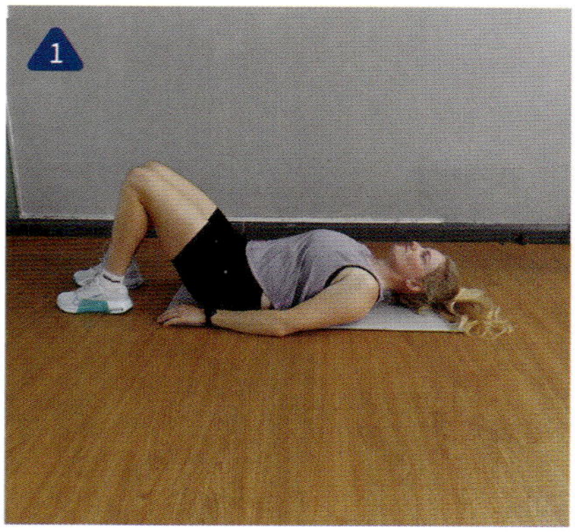

1. Lie on your back with your knees bent

2. Curl up and touch your ankle – alternating sides

A.7. Side Crunch

Purpose: Develops side-bending strength through the obliques.
Equipment: Gym bench.
Recommended Training: 3 sets of 10-15 repetitions per side.
How To Do It: Lie on one side on a flat padded gym bench, gripping the bench with your feet for stability. With hands loosely touching opposite shoulders, lift the shoulder off the bench / flex the side of your trunk – the movement range is fairly small. Speed: 1 second up; no hold; 1 second down. Change sides.

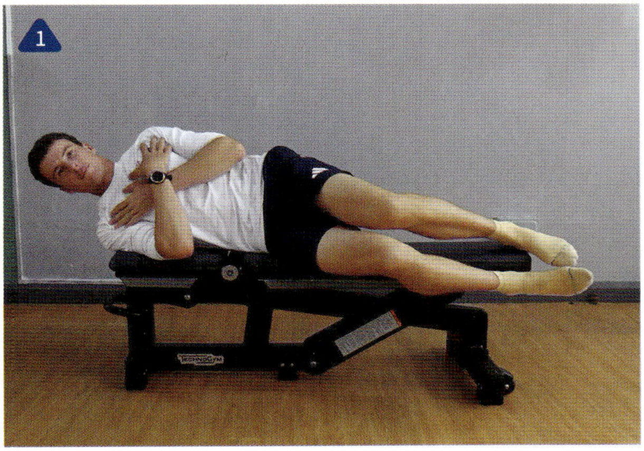

1. Lie on one side on a padded bench with your feet wrapped round either side of the bench

2. Lift the shoulders slightly off the bench

A.8. Medicine Ball Side Passes

Purpose: Builds rotational power and control through the trunk, useful for manoeuvres like roll tacks and roll gybes.
Equipment: Medicine ball and wall or partner.
Recommended Training: 2-3 sets of 10-15 throws per side.
How To Do It: Seated or standing, side-on to a wall or your partner, throw a medicine ball (2-5kg) forcefully to a wall or partner and catch it on return. Maintain posture and core engagement.

1. Sit side-on to your partner or a wall with a medicine ball

2. Throw the medicine ball to your partner or against the wall

3. Who throws it back

4. Catch it, while maintaining posture and core engagement

A.9. Crucifix

(See p49)

Purpose: Strengthens the obliques and deep stabilisers through controlled rotation of the legs.
Equipment: None.
Recommended Training: 3 sets of 8-12.
How To Do It: Lie on your back with arms extended to the sides and legs pointing upward. Lower the legs together to one side, then the other, keeping shoulders on the floor. Speed: 3 seconds from feet on one side to feet the other side.

Lower your legs together to one side

A.10. Reverse Sit-Up

(See p46, 47)

Purpose: Strengthens lower core with emphasis on lifting the pelvis.
Equipment: None.
Recommended Training: 3-4 sets of 10-15 repetitions.
How To Do It: Lie flat with knees slightly bent, hands lightly behind your head. Lift both feet and hips off the floor, curling the pelvis upward before lowering slowly. Speed: 1 second up; no hold; 2 seconds down.

Lift both feet and hips off the floor

A.11. V-Sits

(See p47)

Purpose: Integrates upper and lower core work; high difficulty.
Equipment: None.
Recommended Training: 2-3 sets of 8-12 repetitions.
How To Do It: From lying flat on your back with your hands lightly behind your head, raise both legs to about 60°, then lift the upper body into a crunch simultaneously to form a 'V' shape. Speed: 1 second up; no hold; 1 second down.

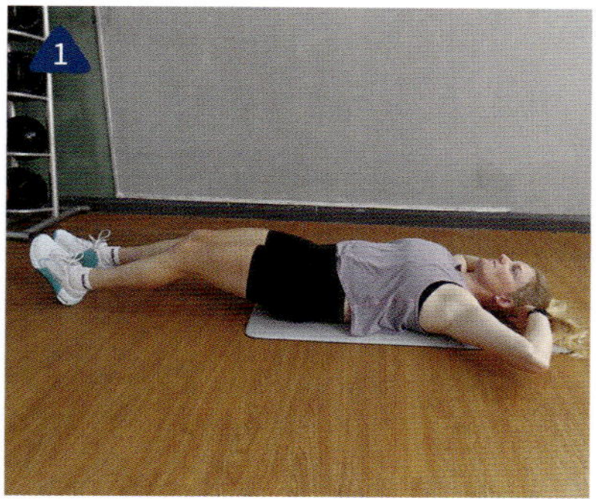

1. Lie flat on your back with your hands lightly behind your head

2. Raise both legs to about 60°

3. Lift the upper body into a crunch to form a 'V' shape

A.12. Single Leg Raise

Purpose: Builds control and endurance through the lower core.
Equipment: None. Incline bench for leg throws variations.
Recommended Training: 3 sets of 10-15 lifts each leg.
How To Do It: Laying down with arms against your side, one leg straight and the other bent, flatten your lower back against the floor, lift the straight leg slowly to about 45°, lower with control. Do the reps, then swap legs. Speed: 2 second up; no hold; 2 seconds down.

1. Lie down, flattening your lower back against the floor with one leg straight and the other bent

2. Lift the straight leg slowly to about 45° and then lower with control

Variations:
Double Leg Raise: Lift both legs at once for a greater challenge.
Leg Throws: Lying face up on an incline bench, hands clasping its top, raise your straight legs hard and fast. A training partner stands at your feet, catching them as they are raised, then throwing them down. The training partner should vary height from which the feet are thrown down.

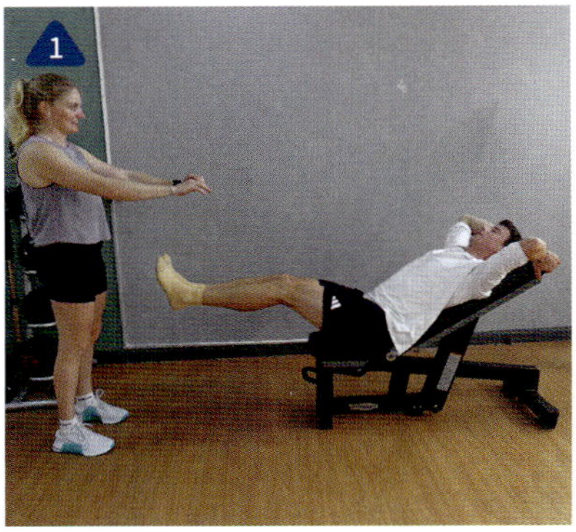

1. Lie face up on an incline bench with straight legs

2. Raise your legs hard and fast, your partner catches them

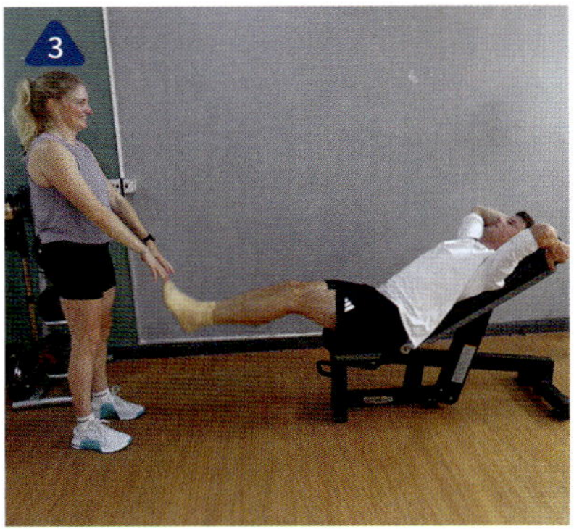

3. And then throws them down

A.13. Hanging Knee Raise

(See p47)

Purpose: Builds lower core and hip flexor strength while promoting trunk stability.

Equipment: Wall bars, hanging bar or elbow rests. Medicine ball for variation.

Recommended Training: 3 sets of 8-10 repetitions.

How To Do It: Hang from a bar or rest on elbow supports, then raise the knees toward the chest in a controlled motion. Speed: 1 second up; no hold; 1 second down.

Variations:

Straight-Leg Raise: Lift extended legs for more challenge.

Medicine Ball Knee Raise: Hold a medicine ball between your knees for added resistance.

1. Hang from a bar

2. Raise your knees towards the chest in a controlled motion

Variation: Straight-Leg Raise

Variation: Medicine Ball Knee Raise

A.14. Wood Chop

(See p40, 41, 49)

Purpose: Develops rotational power and trunk control through the obliques and hips – ideal for roll tacks, gybes and sheeting actions that combine twist and drive.

Equipment: Medicine ball, cable or resistance band.

Recommended Training: 3 sets of 10-15 repetitions each side.

How To Do It: Stand with feet shoulder-width apart, holding a cable handle, resistance band or medicine ball high to one side. In one smooth motion, pull or swing the weight diagonally across your body toward the opposite hip, rotating through the trunk and hips. Control the return to the start position. Keep your arms straight but not locked, and maintain a strong, stable stance. Speed: 1 second down; no hold; 2 seconds up.

1. Stand with feet shoulder-width apart, holding a cable handle, resistance band or medicine ball high to one side

2. In one smooth motion, pull or swing the weight diagonally across your body toward the opposite hip, rotating through the trunk and hips

Tip: Imagine you're pulling in a sheet or swinging a boom across – power through the core, not the arms.

Variation: Half-Kneeling Wood Chop

Variations:

Low-to-High Wood Chop: Start near the opposite knee and lift diagonally upward to finish above the opposite shoulder.

Half-Kneeling Wood Chop: Perform the same motion while kneeling on one knee for extra core control and balance.

A.15. Pallof Press

(See p15, 39, 41, 79, 90)

Purpose: Builds anti-rotation strength through the deep core muscles, teaching the trunk to stay stable under load. It complements the Wood Chop by training control and resistance rather than power in rotation.

Equipment: Cable or resistance band.

Recommended Training: 3 sets of 8-12 controlled presses each side.

How To Do It: Stand side-on to a cable or resistance band anchored at chest height. Hold the handle or band against your chest, step out for tension, then press your hands straight forward over 1 second without letting your torso twist. Pause briefly, then return slowly over 1 second. Begin with a light load and progress to a resistance that is challenging while maintaining control.

Tip: Imagine you're bracing against the pull of a kite sheet in a gust – solid, centred, no rotation.

1. Stand side-on to a cable or resistance band anchored at chest height. Hold the handle or band against your chest

2. Press your hands straight forward without letting your torso twist. Pause, then return slowly

Variations:

Half-Kneeling Pallof Press: Conduct the same exercise but kneeling on one knee. Adds a balance challenge.

Overhead Pallof Press: Start in the same position but instead of pressing your hands forward, press them upwards. Increases shoulder engagement.

Variation: Half-Kneeling Pallof Press

Variation: Overhead Pallof Press

A.16. Russian Twist

Purpose: Builds rotational strength and control through the obliques – important for tacks, gybes and body rotation.

Equipment: None. Medicine ball and gym ball, back-extension bench or hiking bench for variations.

Recommended Training: 3 sets of 10-16 twists.

How To Do It: From a half-sit-up position, hold your torso at 45° and rotate the trunk fully side to side. Add a medicine ball or weight for extra resistance.

Variation: Hiking Twist: In a hiking position on a back-extension bench or ball with your feet anchored, hold a medicine ball and rotate fully side to side, mimicking hiking rotation.

1. Start in a half sit-up position, with your torso at 45°

2. Rotate the trunk fully to one side, then the other

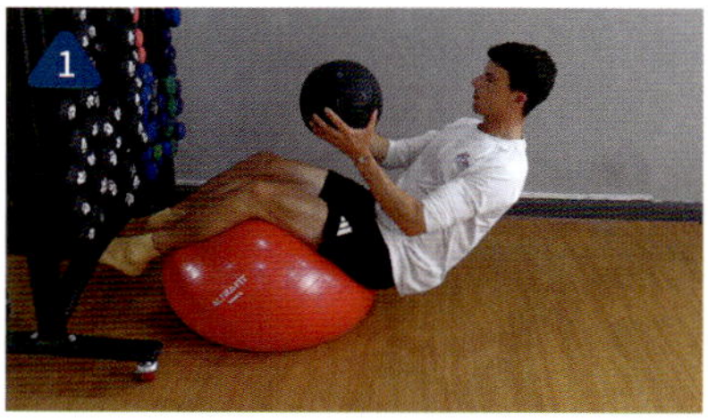

1. Start in a hiking position on a gym ball, with your torso at 45°

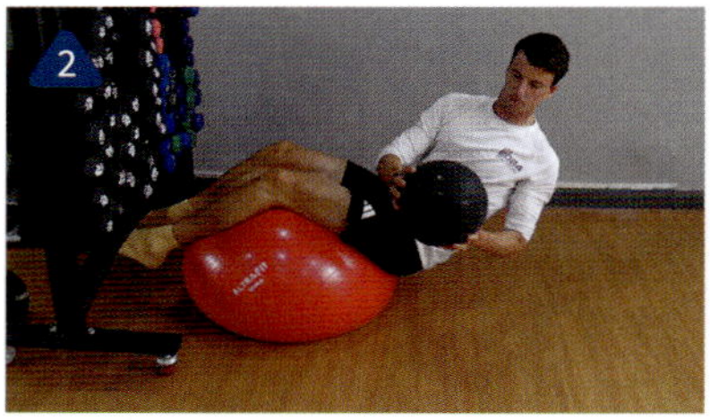

2. Rotate the trunk fully to one side, then the other

A.17. Forearm Plank

(See p70, 74, 76, 82, 90)

Purpose: Strengthens deep core stabilisers and reinforces posture control for hiking and sheeting.

Equipment: None. Small ball for variation.

Recommended Training: 3 sets of 20-40-second holds, resting 10-20 seconds between. Gradually extend hold time as you improve. Of course, you can alter the work to rest interval to suit.

How To Do It: Lie face-down on a mat, resting on forearms and toes. Keep the body flat and core tight. Avoid letting hips drop or rise.

Variation: Forearm Plank with Feet on Ball: As above, but with a small gym or medicine ball under the toes to add instability.

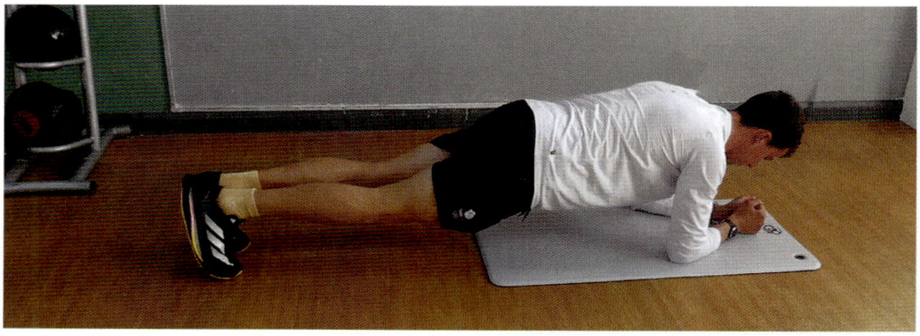

Forearm plank

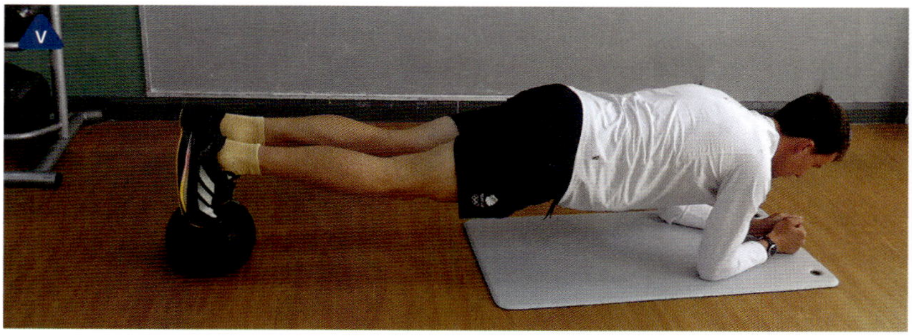

Variation: Forearm plank with feet on ball

Scan to watch video

B. Gym Ball Exercises

These exercises add controlled instability to your training, improving balance, posture and coordination. They help develop the small stabilising muscles that support many movements or static holds while sailing.

B.1. Prone Alternate Arm & Leg

(See p75, 90)

Purpose: Strengthens trunk stabilisers and improves body control when reaching or moving asymmetrically – similar to balancing during manoeuvres.

Equipment: Gym ball.

Recommended Training: 2 sets of 10-15 repetitions each side.

How To Do It: Lie face-down on the ball with your stomach centred and both hands and feet on the floor. Lift one arm and the opposite leg just above ball height, pause briefly, then lower and switch sides. Keep hips level and core braced throughout.

1. Lie face-down on the ball with your stomach centred and both hands and feet on the floor

2. Lift one arm and the opposite leg just above ball height, pause briefly, then lower and switch sides

B.2. Seated Single Leg

(See p90)

Purpose: Trains balance and core activation while seated – valuable for posture control in light-wind conditions.

Equipment: Gym ball.

Recommended Training: 3 sets of 10-second holds per leg.

How To Do It: Sit tall on the ball with both feet on the floor. Engage your core ('draw in' the stomach). Lift one foot and hold steady for 10 seconds without letting the ball wobble (much). Switch legs each set. 3 x 10 seconds x 2 legs makes it a ~60-second exercise.

1. Sit tall on the ball with both feet on the floor

2. Engage your core and lift one leg and hold steady without letting the ball wobble

B.3. Prone Hand Walk

(See p49)

Purpose: Builds whole-body stability and shoulder strength through movement – useful for maintaining control during position changes in the boat.

Equipment: Gym ball.

Recommended Training: 2 sets of 4-6 walks forward and back.

How To Do It: Lie chest-down on the ball, feet on the floor. Roll forward until your hands touch the floor, then walk forward on your hands until the feet are fully on the ball, then reverse. Keep the trunk firm and hips level. Speed: 2-3 seconds to walk out (no pause) and 2-3 seconds to walk back.

1. Lie chest down on the ball with your feet on the floor

2. Roll forward until your hands touch the floor

3. Walk forward on your hands until your feet are fully on the ball, then reverse

B.4. Side Bend In Side Lying

Purpose: Strengthens the obliques and lateral stabilisers that help resist side-leaning and twisting under load.

Equipment: Gym ball.

Recommended Training: 2 sets of 8-10 repetitions per side.

How To Do It: Lie on your side with both feet resting on a ball. Support yourself on the lower elbow, with your upper hand holding a wall bar. Lift your hips to create a straight line from shoulders to ankles. Lower and raise the hips in a slow, controlled motion. Speed: About 1 second up and 1 second down – it's a short range of motion exercise.

1. Lie on your side with both feet resting on a ball. Support yourself on the lower elbow, with your upper hand holding a wall bar

2. Lift your hips to create a straight line from shoulders to ankle

B.5. Prone Single-Leg Off

(See p90)

Purpose: Develops trunk control, shoulder stability and hip strength in a prone position.

Equipment: Gym ball.

Recommended Training: 2 sets of 8-10 repetitions each leg.

How To Do It: Begin in a push-up position with toes on the ball and hands on the floor. Lift one leg slowly out to the side over five seconds, keeping hips square, then return and repeat with the other leg. Keep the body straight and steady.

1. Begin in a push-up position with toes on the ball and hands on the floor

2. Lift one leg slowly out to the side over five seconds, keeping hips square, then return and repeat with the other leg

C. Chest & Triceps Exercises

Scan to watch video

While upper body pushing strength isn't a primary need in sailing, developing the chest and triceps helps balance the muscles used for pulling, improves shoulder stability and supports movements like handling spinnaker poles, mainsheet trimming and bracing during manoeuvres.

C.1. Push-Ups

(See p15, 49, 74, 75, 76, 81, 82)

Purpose: Builds general upper-body strength in the chest, shoulders and triceps, while engaging the core for body alignment.

Equipment: None. Gym ball and wallbars for variations.

Recommended Training: 2-3 sets of 8-15 repetitions. Adjust difficulty to maintain full control through each rep.

How To Do It: Start prone with hands slightly wider than shoulder width and toes on the ground. Keep the body straight from head to heels. Lower the chest to just above the floor, then push up until arms are straight. Speed: 3 seconds down, no pause, then 1 second up.

1. Start in the prone position with your hands on the floor slightly wider than shoulder width and toes on the ground

2. Keeping the body straight from head to heels, lower the chest to just above the floor, then push up until arms are straight

Variation: Feet On Gym Ball Push-up

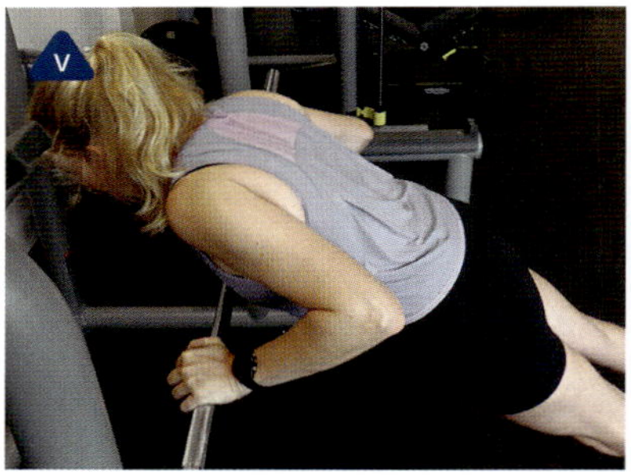

Variation: Push-Up Against A Bar

Variations:

Knees On The Floor Push-Ups: The same exercise, but with your knees on the ground. Easier for beginners.

Feet Elevated Push-Ups: The same exercise, but with your feet elevated. Increases load on the upper chest and shoulders.

Feet On Gym Ball Push-Ups: As before but with your feet elevated on a gym ball. Adds core stability challenge.

Push-Ups Against A Wall or Bar: Standing up, leaning against a wall or barwith your hands on the wall or bar. Allows higher repetition practice for technique and endurance.

C.2. Bench Press (Bar Or Dumbbell)

(See p15, 34, 49)

Purpose: Strengthens the chest, shoulders and triceps; contributes to balanced upper-body development and supports force transfer when stabilising or bracing the arms under load.

Equipment: Barbell or dumbbells and bench – flat for basic exercise, incline or decline for variations.

Recommended Training: 3-4 sets of 6-10 repetitions with a controlled tempo. If you're new to the exercise, start with a total load of around 20% of your body weight (barbell plus plates, or combined dumbbell weight) for the 6-10 rep range. If you can comfortably exceed 10 reps, increase the load in small increments until 10 reps is challenging. Use a spotter for heavier lifts. For most sailors, there is little benefit in building bench press strength beyond the ability to perform 10 controlled reps at body-weight load.

How To Do It: Lying on a flat bench, hold the bar slightly wider than shoulder width. Lower slowly to just above the chest, then push strongly to full extension. Keep feet on the floor and back flat. Speed: 3 seconds down, no pause, 1 second up.

Variations:

Decline Bench Press: Performed on a bench angled downwards. Targets lower chest.

Incline Bench Press: Performed on a bench angled upwards. Places greater emphasis on shoulders and upper chest.

Bar Bench Press

Dumbbell Bench Press: This develops each arm independently and improves balance between sides

Variation: Decline Bench Press

Variation: Incline Bench Press

C.3. Dips

Purpose: Builds strength through the triceps, shoulders and lower chest, improving pushing power and shoulder stability.

Equipment: Dip bars.

Recommended Training: 2 sets of 8-10 repetitions. Partial range can be used as you fatigue.

How To Do It: Grasp dip bars and lift yourself to straight-arm position, then lower until elbows reach about 90°. Push back to full extension. Keep the body upright to emphasise triceps or lean slightly forward to recruit more chest. Speed: 2 seconds down, no pause, 1 second up.

1. Lift yourself to the straight-arm position

2. Lower until the elbows reach about 90°

Scan to watch video

D. Leg Exercises

Developing strong legs is vital for hiking endurance and overall stability in sailing. These large muscles also play a major role in weight gain for lighter sailors aiming to increase body mass. Strong legs help maintain hiking posture longer and transfer power effectively from upper body to boat.

D.1. Leg Extension

(See p30, 49)

Purpose: Builds quadriceps strength and endurance for hiking.

Equipment: Leg extension machine.

Recommended Training: 3-4 sets of 8-12 repetitions with controlled effort on both the lift and the return. Because leg extension machines vary widely in geometry and friction, the indicated weight can differ significantly between machines. Start conservatively and adjust by feel, aiming for a load where 12 full-range repetitions are challenging but still well controlled.

1. Sit in the machine with your ankles against the pads

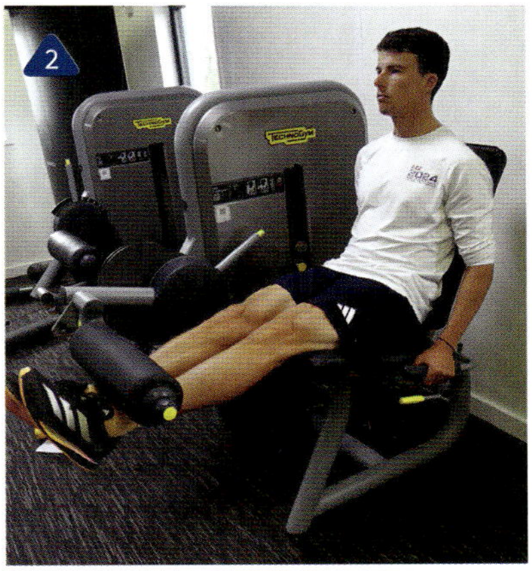

2. Extend your legs smoothly to full extension, pause briefly, then lower under control

How To Do It: Sit in the machine with ankles against the pad. Extend the legs smoothly to full extension, pause briefly, then lower under control without letting the weight stack touch. Speed: 1 second up, no pause, 1 second down.

Variations:

Limited Range of Motion Leg Extension: Work through only the last 15-20° of movement to target straighter-leg hiking angles.

Single-Leg Extension: Perform one leg at a time using slightly less than half the two-leg load to correct imbalances.

Variation: Single-Leg Extension

D.2. Leg Press

(See p15, 30, 49)

Purpose: Strengthens quadriceps, glutes and hamstrings, improving power in hiking and manoeuvres.

Equipment: Leg press machine.

Recommended Training: 3-4 sets of 7-10 repetitions. Use a moderate to heavy load with steady control. Again, these machines can vary widely in geometry and friction, so weights can feel significantly different between machines. Start conservatively and adjust by feel, aiming for a load where 12 full-range repetitions are challenging but still well controlled.

How To Do It: Adjust the seat so knees are bent at 90° at the start. Push the platform away until legs are nearly straight (but not locked), then lower smoothly until knees are again at 90°. Keep the lower back pressed into the seat. Speed: Push over 2 seconds, slight pause, ease down for 2 seconds.

Variations:
Limited Range of Motion Leg Press: Work only through the final 15-20° to simulate hiking angles.
Single-Leg Press: Use roughly half your normal load to strengthen each leg individually.

1. Start with the knees bent at 90°

2. Push the platform away until the knees are nearly straight, then lower smoothly until knees are again at 90°

Variation: Single leg press

D.3. Squats

(See p15, 30, 33, 41, 49, 74, 76, 80, 82)
Purpose: The most complete lower-body strength exercise. Builds power through the quadriceps, glutes and hamstrings, supporting hiking endurance and movement control.
Equipment: Barbell, plates and squat rack. Smith machine and dumbbells for variations.
Recommended Training: 3-4 sets of 8-10 repetitions. Prioritise technique before adding weight. As a broad guide, aim to work toward a squat load of around 50-75% of body weight for controlled sets of 8-10 repetitions. If you are new to squatting, begin with body weight only or ~20-40% of body weight and build gradually. More experienced or stronger sailors may progress beyond body-weight loading, but only while maintaining consistent technique, full range of motion and control.

1. Position the bar across the shoulders, feet shoulder-width apart, toes slightly out

2. Bend at the knees and hips together, keeping the chest out, until the thighs are about parallel to the floor, then drive upward strongly

How To Do It: With supervision, if possible, position the bar across the shoulders (not the neck). Feet shoulder-width apart, toes slightly out. Bend at knees and hips together, keeping chest up and knees tracking over toes. Lower until thighs are about parallel to the floor (90° at the knees), then drive upward strongly. Speed: Down for 2 seconds; no pause then drive up over 1 second. Pause briefly at the top to stabilise.

Variations:
Split Squat: Step one foot forward into a split stance (around 50-70cm, depending on height). Lower under control by bending both knees, dropping the rear knee toward the ground while keeping the torso upright. Drive back to standing by extending both legs, maintaining even pressure through the feet. Improves leg strength, balance and lower-body control.
Squat On Smith Machine: Using a Smith Machine offers guided movement for learning or added safety.
Dumbbell Squat: Hold weights at your sides or hugged to your chest if shoulder or neck discomfort prevents barbell use.

Variation: Squat On Smith Machine

Variation: Dumbbell Split Squat

D.4. Step-Ups
(See p81, 82)
Purpose: Builds functional single-leg strength, balance and control similar to roll tacking and moving across the boat.
Equipment: Dumbbells and bench.
Recommended Training: 2 sets of 10-12 repetitions each leg. Begin with body weight only as a warm-up, then add load progressively. As a broad guide, work toward a total external load of around 10-30% of body weight, typically split evenly between two dumbbells. Start at the lower end of the range and increase only while maintaining balance, control and consistent step height.
How To Do It: Stand facing a bench or box about 40cm high, holding dumbbells. Step up with one foot, fully extend the leg, then step back down with the same leg. Complete all reps on one side before switching. Speed: Up in 1 second, down in 1 second.

1. Stand facing a bench or box about 40cm high holding dumbbells

2. Step up with one foot

3. Fully extend the leg, then step back down

D.5. Romanian Deadlift (RDL)

(See p15, 41, 79)

Purpose: Strengthens the hamstrings, glutes and spinal stabilisers – key for hip power, hiking endurance and injury prevention.

Equipment: Dumbbells or barbell.

Recommended Training: 3-4 sets of 6-10 repetitions. Load guidance: Use a relatively light load – typically around 20-50% of bodyweight – that allows you to maintain a neutral spine and feel a strong stretch through the hamstrings on every repetition. This is not a maximal lift; prioritise control and quality of movement over the weight lifted.

How To Do It: Stand tall with a barbell or dumbbells in front of the thighs (hands slightly wider than the legs). Keeping the back straight and knees slightly bent, hinge forward at the hips over 2-3 seconds until you feel tension in the hamstrings. Drive the hips forward to return upright in about 2 seconds. Keep the dumbbell / bar close to the legs throughout.

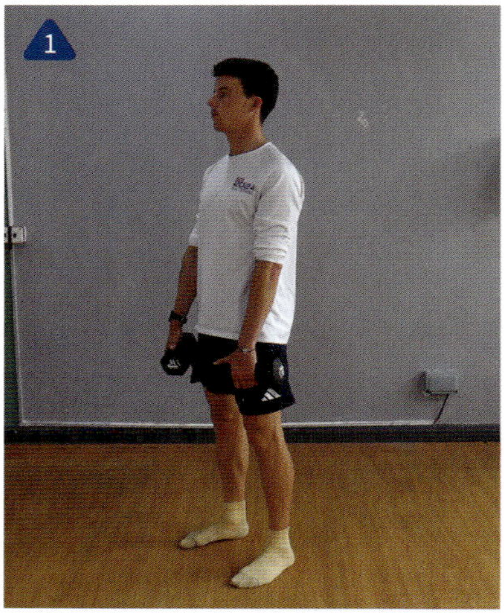

1. Stand tall with the dumbbells in front of the thighs

2. Keeping the back straight and knees bent, hinge forward at the hips until you feel tension in the hamstrings. Drive the hips forward to return upright

Tip: Think 'hips back, hips forward', not 'bend the knees'. This is about controlled stretch and drive.

D.6. Hiking Leg Extensions

(See p48)

Purpose: Mimics the specific knee-extension movement of hiking, improving endurance at near-locked angles.

Equipment: Gym ball, back-extension or hiking bench.

Recommended Training: 2-3 sets of 12-20 repetitions.

How To Do It: Sit in a hiking posture on a gym ball or back-extension bench with your feet anchored and arms by your side or on your chest. Extend the legs through the final few degrees of motion and relax back. Leaning further back increases resistance. Speed: These can be done at a pace of 1 second up, 1 second down.

1. Sit in a hiking position on a gym ball with your feet anchored and arms by your side or on your chest

2. Extend the legs through the final few degrees of motion and relax back

D.7. Toe Curls

Purpose: Strengthens the small muscles of the feet and ankles, supporting hiking.

Equipment: Dumbbells or barbell.

Recommended Training: 2 sets of 10-12 repetitions. Start with around 5kg per foot and adjust the load to provide a clear but controllable challenge.

How To Do It: Sit on the floor with toes positioned under dumbbells (or a barbell) and knees bent. Flex the toes upward (1 second) and downward (1 second) through a full range. A small support under the heels may help maintain motion. Some balancing of the dumbbells is required and is part of the challenge.

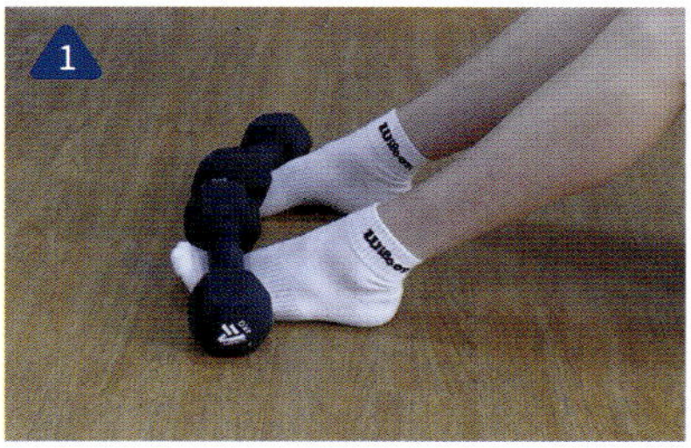

1. Sit on the floor with the toes positioned under dumbbells and knees bent

2. Flex the toes upward and downward through a full range

D.8. Lateral Bound With Controlled Landing

(See p33)

Purpose: Develops lateral power, leg strength and landing control. Particularly relevant for dynamic balance, shock absorption and rapid changes of direction on the boat.

Equipment: None.

Recommended Training: 2-3 sets of 12-20 controlled landings each side. Quality over speed.

How To Do It: Stand on one leg. Bound laterally to the opposite side, landing softly on the other foot. On landing, absorb the force by bending slightly at the hip, knee and ankle, keeping the knee tracking over the toes. Hold the landing briefly to regain full control before rebounding back.

Coaching Cues: Land quietly. Control first, power second. If the landing cannot be stabilised, reduce the distance.

Variations:

Shorter hops: Focusing purely on landing control.

Continuous: Side-to-side bounds for more elastic emphasis (only once control is established).

1. Start balanced on one leg

2. Bound laterally to the opposite side

3. Land under control, stabilise before rebounding

D.9. Single-Leg Balance

(See p33, 40, 41)

Purpose: Improves balance, ankle and hip stability, and postural control. Supports efficient force transfer and reduces injury risk during hiking, manoeuvres and unstable deck movement.

Equipment: None. BOSU ball or wobble board for variation.

Recommended Training: 2-3 sets of 20-40 seconds per leg.

How To Do It: Stand tall on one leg with a slight bend at the knee. Maintain balance while keeping hips level and posture relaxed. The non-standing leg should be held off the ground without excessive tension. Increase difficulty via the variations below once stable balance can be maintained.

Variations:

BOSU ball or wobble board

Eyes closed

Add arm exercise: Light upper-body movement or simulated sail-handling actions.

Knee bend: Add a greater knee bend and hold.

Single-leg balance on stable ground

Variation: Single-leg balance with knee bend

D.10. Calf Raises

(See p34, 40)

Purpose: Builds calf strength and endurance for sustained trapezing, particularly through the ankle and lower leg stabilisers that support prolonged loading and micro-adjustments.

Equipment: None.

Recommended Training: 2-3 sets of 12-20 repetitions. Move smoothly and with control.

How To Do It: Stand tall with the balls of the feet on the edge of a step or block, heels free. Rise up onto the toes (1 second), pause briefly at the top, then lower the heels under control (1 second) to a comfortable stretch. Use a handrail or wall lightly for balance if needed.

Coaching Cues: Move through a full range. Control the lowering phase. Avoid bouncing.

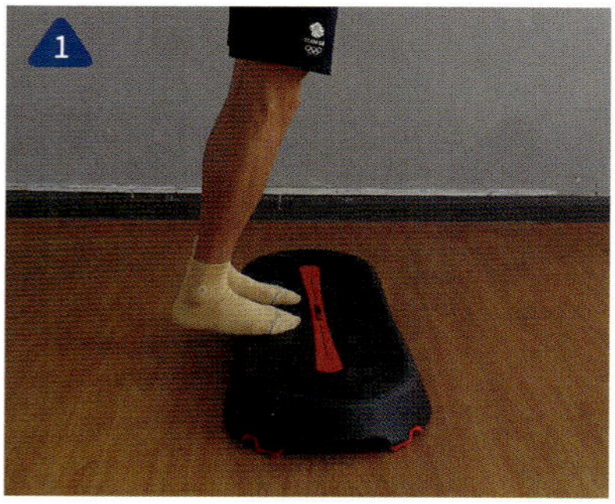

1. Start with the heels lowered over the edge of the step

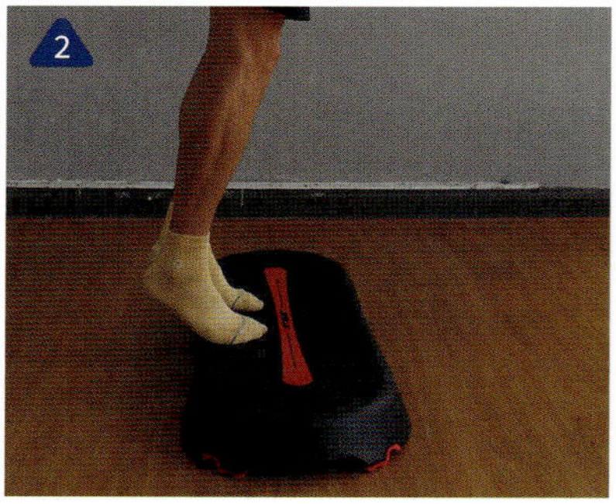

2. Rise smoothly onto the toes, pause briefly, then lower under control

Variations:

Single-Leg Calf Raise: Perform on one leg at a time using bodyweight or light external load.

Single-Leg Calf Hold: Rise onto one foot and hold the top position for 20-40 seconds to develop endurance specific to trapezing.

Bent-Knee Calf Raise: Slight knee bend to increase soleus involvement.

Scan to watch video

E. Upper Back & Bicep

The upper back, shoulders and biceps are central to your sheeting and pumping power. These muscles stabilise the shoulders, control the sails and resist fatigue during repeated actions. Building balanced pulling strength also helps protect the shoulders and elbows from overuse injuries.

E.1. Lat Pull-Down

(See p39, 49)

Purpose: Develops strength through the latissimus dorsi, shoulders and biceps – the key muscles for sheeting and pulling actions.

Equipment: Lat Pull-Down Machine. Towel for variation.

Recommended Training: 3-4 sets of 8-12 repetitions. Begin at around half your body weight. If you can complete all sets comfortably with strict technique, increase the load gradually; if you're forced to lean back or use momentum, reduce the load.

How To Do It: Sit upright and grasp the bar slightly wider than shoulder width. Pull the bar down smoothly to chin or upper chest level, then control the return to full arm extension. Keep the trunk stable and avoid swinging. Speed: Down for 1-2 seconds, brief pause, then up for 3 seconds.

Variations:

U-Bar Grip Lat Pull-Down: Use a narrower grip to shift emphasis toward biceps.

Behind Neck Lat Pull-Down: Pull to the back of the neck (only with excellent mobility and control).

Leaning Back Lat Pull-Down: Lean trunk to ~45° and pull to the chest for a stronger power phase.

Towel Grip Lat Pull-Down: Wrap a towel around the bar to challenge grip and forearm endurance.

1. Sit upright and grasp the bar slightly wider than shoulder width

2. Pull the bar down smoothly to chin or upper chest level, then control the return to full arm extension

Variation: U-Bar (narrow) Grip Lat Pull-Down

Variation: Behind Neck Lat Pull-Down

Variation: Leaning Back Lat Pull-Down

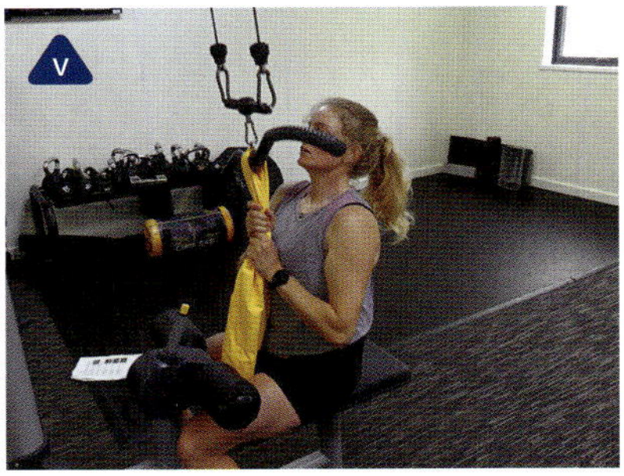

Variation: Towel Grip Lat Pull-Down

E.2. Chin-Up

(See p15, 33, 46, 76)

Purpose: Builds powerful pulling strength and endurance for sheeting, trapezing and pumping.

Equipment: Chin-up bar. Towel, bench and medicine ball for variations.

Recommended Training: 3-4 sets to near fatigue (usually 5-12 repetitions). Adjust assistance or add load to hit the rep range while maintaining good form.

How To Do It: Grasp an overhead bar shoulder-width apart, palms forward. Pull the body upward until the chin clears the bar, then lower slowly to straight arms. Keep the body stable and avoid swinging. Speed: 1 second up, no pause, 2 seconds down.

1. Grasp an overhead bar shoulder width apart, palms forward

2. Pull the body upward until the chin clears the bar, then lower slowly to straight arms

Variations:

Towel or Rope Grip Chin-Up: Gripping a towel or rope wrapped around the bar improves forearm and grip strength.

Assisted Chin-Up: For a slightly easier exercise, use a long rubber band or place toes on a bench for partial support.

Weighted Chin-Up: Hold a medicine ball between the legs for added resistance.

Iron Cross Chin-Up: Raise legs horizontally while performing chin-ups for advanced trunk engagement.

Variation: Towel Grip Chin-Up

Variation: Assisted Chin-Up with rubber band

Variation: Iron Cross Chin-Up with legs raised horizontally

E.3. Seated Row

(See p39, 41, 49, 80, 81, 82)

Purpose: Strengthens mid-back muscles (rhomboids, trapezius, lats) for powerful and controlled sheeting and pumping.

Equipment: Rowing machine. Towel for variation.

Recommended Training: 3-4 sets of 8-12 repetitions. Select a load that allows you to complete all reps with a tall, stable trunk, finishing each set with 2-3 repetitions in reserve. As a guide, this is often around 50-70% of body weight on a cable machine. Increase the load only once posture and control are maintained throughout.

How To Do It: Sit tall with knees slightly bent. Pull handles toward your waist, squeezing shoulder blades together at the end, then return smoothly to full extension without leaning forward. Speed: 1 second pull, slight pause, 2 second ease.

Variations:

One-Arm Seated Row: Complete the rowing movement with one arm, being careful not to overload one side of the body. This focuses on unilateral strength and control.

Towel Grip Seated Row: Gripping a towel wrapped around the handles enhances grip endurance.

Scapular Retraction Seated Row: A shorter-range movement. Keeping the arms roughly straight, squeeze the shoulder blades (scapular) together firmly and then let the shoulders go forward again.

1. Sit tall with knees slightly bent

2. Pull the handles towards your waist, squeezing the shoulder blades together at the end

Variation: One-Arm Seated Row

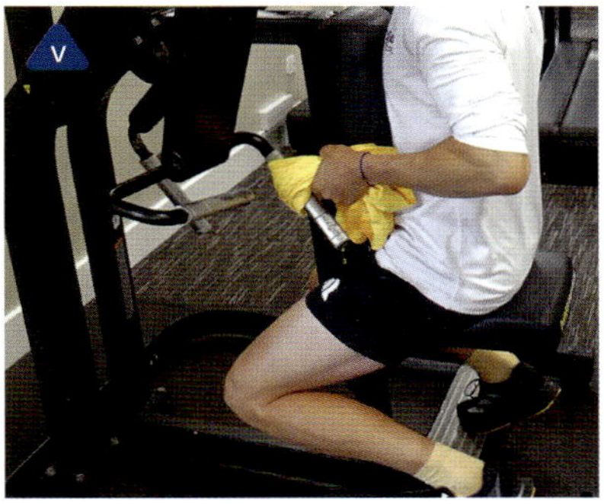

Variation: Towel Grip Seated Row

Variation: Scapular Retraction seated: 1. Start as usual

2. Squeeze the shoulder blades together

E.4. Towel Dead Hang

(See p33, 34, 39)

Purpose: Develops forearm and grip endurance – vital for long sheeting efforts and pumping endurance. Also strengthens shoulder stabilisers and improves postural endurance.

Equipment: Chin-up bar and towel.

Recommended Training: 3-4 sets of 20-40-second hangs. Rest 60-90 seconds between sets.

How To Do It: Drape a towel over a chin-up bar and grasp both ends firmly. Hang with arms straight, shoulders engaged and body still. Avoid swinging or letting the shoulders shrug up toward your ears.

> **Tip: Focus on smooth breathing and a relaxed jaw – the grip should feel firm but not frantic.**

Towel Dead Hang

E.5. Body-Weight Pull-Ups (Horizontal Row)

(See p33, 42, 48, 49, 70, 75, 81)

Purpose: Builds back and arm endurance with lower load – ideal for those without access to machines.

Equipment: Low horizontal bar or table edge.

Recommended Training: 3 sets of 10-15 repetitions.

How To Do It: Lie under a low bar or sturdy table edge. With hands shoulder-width apart, pull the chest up to touch the bar, then lower slowly. Keep the body straight and core engaged. Speed: Pull up over 1 second, no pause, lower over 2 seconds.

1. Lie under a low bar, gripping it with hands shoulder-width apart

2. Pull the chest up to touch the bar, then lower slowly

E.6. Bench Row

(See p34, 49)

Purpose: Strengthens the upper back and posterior shoulders with a stable trunk position.

Equipment: Dumbbells or barbell and high bench.

Recommended Training: 4 sets of 8-12 repetitions. Begin with a weight of around 30% of body weight and increase gradually once all sets can be completed with strict control and no loss of range.

How To Do It: Lie face-down on a high bench holding dumbbells or a barbell. Pull the weight up to touch the underside of the bench then lower under control. Speed: 1 second up, no pause and 2 seconds down.

1. Lie face-down on a high bench holding a barbell or dumbbells

2. Pull the weight toward the underside of the bench, pause briefly, then lower under control

E.7. One-Arm Dumbbell Row

Purpose: Develops unilateral pulling strength and trunk stability for asymmetrical movements like main and jib sheeting.

Equipment: Dumbbell and bench.

Recommended Training: 2 sets of 8-12 repetitions per arm. Begin with a weight around 15-20% of body weight and increase only once you can complete all reps with strict control and no rotation through the torso.

How To Do It: With one knee and hand on a bench, hold a dumbbell in the opposite hand. Pull it smoothly toward your ribs over 1 second, keeping the trunk steady, then lower slowly over 2 seconds.

1. With one knee and hand on a bench, hold a dumbbell in the opposite hand

2. Pull the dumbbell towards your ribs, keeping the trunk steady, then lower slowly

E.8. Upright Row

Purpose: Strengthens the upper trapezius and deltoids, aiding shoulder stability and sheet control under load.

Equipment: Dumbbells or barbell.

Recommended Training: 2-3 sets of 8-12 repetitions. Use a light – moderate load (10-30% body weight total). Prioritise smooth, pain-free movement over heavy resistance.

How To Do It: Stand with a barbell or dumbbells at thigh height. Pull vertically to near the chin, keeping elbows high. Avoid trunk movement or jerking the weight. Speed: 1 second up and 2 seconds down, no pause.

1. Stand with a barbell or dumbbells at thigh height

2. Pull vertically to near the chin, keeping elbows high. Avoid trunk movement or jerking the weight

E.9. Rowing Machine – Sheeting

(See p50)

Purpose: Builds sailing-specific endurance and power through the sheeting motion.

Equipment: Rowing machine.

Recommended Training: 3 sets of 10-15 repetitions or 30-60 seconds continuous effort. Switch hands every 6 pulls. Use a low resistance setting (e.g. Concept2 damper at 1-3).

How To Do It: On a rowing erg, pull the handle with one hand toward one side of the waist rather than centrally. Keep the shoulder low and controlled, mimicking a strong sheeting pull or pump. You might like to pretend that you are 'elbowing' a punching bag behind you. Once the flywheel is moving, aim for a smooth rhythm of about 1 second pull and 1 second ease. Common faults include shrugging the shoulder, pulling across the body, excessive trunk rotation, using too much resistance, or a jerky pull–return rhythm.

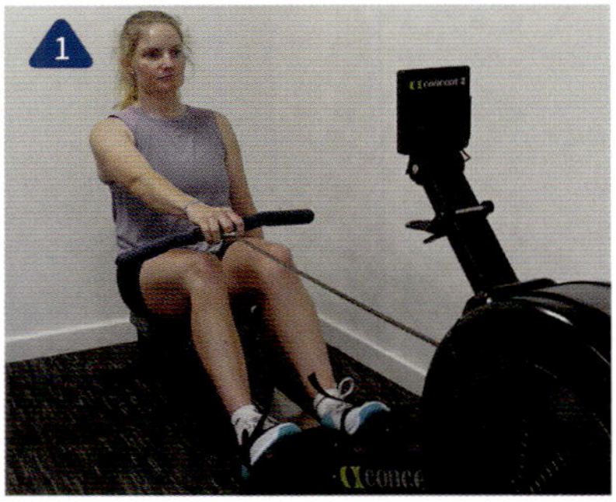

1. On a rowing erg, hold the handle with one hand

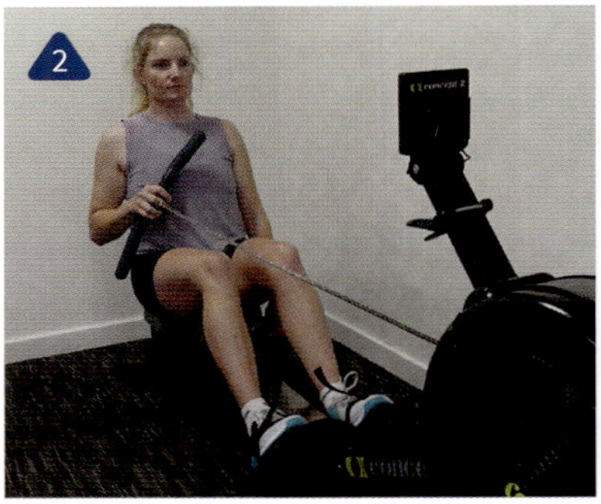

2. Pull the handle toward one side of the waist, keeping the shoulder low and controlled

E.10. Bicep Curl

(See p49)

Purpose: Strengthens the elbow flexors for repeated sheeting and control under load.

Equipment: Dumbbells or barbell. Cable for variation.

Recommended Training: 2 sets of 8-12 repetitions. Use a load you can curl smoothly for 10-12 reps with 2-3 reps in reserve (15-25% body weight total).

How To Do It: Stand with feet shoulder-width apart, barbell or dumbbells in hand. Keep elbows close to your sides and curl the weight upward in a smooth arc. Lower under control. Avoid swinging the body. Speed: 1 second up, 1-2 seconds down, slight pause at the bottom.

Variations:

Alternating Dumbbell Curl: Alternate arms; helps correct strength imbalances.

Hammer Curl: Hold dumbbells with palms facing in, mimicking a natural sheeting grip.

Cable Curl: Provides constant tension through the full movement range. Stand facing the cable in a split stance (one foot slightly forward) to improve balance and limit body sway, core braced. Keep elbows close to your sides and curl smoothly without leaning back or letting the shoulders rise. Use a lighter load than free weights and prioritise control.

1. Stand with feet shoulder-width apart, barbell in hand

2. Keep elbows close to your sides and curl the weight upward in a smooth arc. Lower under control

Variation: Alternating Dumbbell Curl alternating arms

Scan to watch video

F. Lower Back Exercises

The lower back muscles play a key role in stabilising the spine, maintaining posture during hiking and transferring power between the upper and lower body. Strengthening these muscles reduces the risk of lower back pain

F.1. Back Extension

(See p75, 90)

Purpose: Strengthens the spinal erectors and glutes, improving trunk stability and endurance for all sailing movements.

Equipment: Gym ball or back-extension bench.

Recommended Training: 3 sets of 10-15 repetitions. Control the movement and avoid extending beyond the line of your body. Start with body weight only and prioritise control and range. Progress by adding a light load held to the chest only once full sets can be completed with a neutral spine and no loss of control. This is an endurance and control exercise, not a maximal strength lift.

How To Do It: Position yourself face down on a back-extension bench or gym ball with your feet anchored and hands lightly behind your head. Lower the trunk slowly, then raise until your body forms a straight line from shoulders to heels. Do not over-arch. A light weight can be held to the chest to increase difficulty. Speed: 1-2 seconds down, no pause, 1-2 seconds up.

Variations:

Swimming Back Extension: From the horizontal position, move one arm overhead at a time as if swimming, maintaining trunk alignment. Add light weights for extra challenge.

Back Extension with Rotation: With hands behind your head, lower and rotate so the right elbow moves toward the left knee, then uncoil and repeat to the opposite side.

1. Position yourself face down on a gym ball with your feet anchored and hands lightly behind your head

2. Lower the trunk slowly, then raise until your body forms a straight line from shoulders to heels

Variation: Swimming Back Extension

Variation: Back Extension With Rotation

F.2. Reverse Back Extension

Purpose: Strengthens the lower back, glutes and hamstrings from the opposite direction to traditional extensions, providing a different stimulus for back development.

Equipment: Back-extension machine or bench.

Recommended Training: 3 sets of 10-15 repetitions. Use body weight only and focus on smooth, controlled movement.

How To Do It: Lie face-down on a back-extension machine or bench facing the opposite way so that your hips are supported and legs hang freely. Raise the legs until in line with the trunk, pause, then lower slowly. Speed: 1 second up, no pause, 1 second down.

1. Lie face-down on a back-extension machine or bench facing the opposite way so that your hips are supported and legs hang freely

2. Raise the legs until in line with the trunk, pause, then lower slowly

F.3. Superman

Purpose: Builds low-load endurance in the back extensors and glutes, helping maintain posture.

Equipment: None.

Recommended Training: 2 sets of 10-15 repetitions or 20-30-second holds.

How To Do It: Lie face-down with arms extended overhead. Lift both arms and legs off the ground simultaneously, holding briefly before lowering – like Superman flying! Keep the neck in line with the spine and movement smooth.

1. Lie face-down with arms extended overhead

2. Lift both arms and legs off the ground simultaneously, holding briefly before lowering

Scan to watch video

G. Shoulder Exercises

Strong, stable shoulders help you handle sheet loads and steer smoothly. These exercises work the deltoids and rotator cuff – the muscles that move and steady the arms. Keep technique light and controlled; it's better to use small weights well than big weights badly.

G.1. Three-Way Shoulder Work

(See p49)

Purpose: Strengthens all parts of the deltoids – front, middle and rear – for balanced shoulder control and posture.

Equipment: Light dumbbells and a high bench.

Recommended Training: 2 sets of 8-12 repetitions in each direction. Start with very light dumbbells (just a few kilograms). Increase gradually only if control is maintained throughout.

How To Do It: Lie face-down on a high bench holding light dumbbells, arms hanging straight down. Lift the arms smoothly forward to bench height, lower under control, then lift out to the side, lower, and finally lift backward, lowering again. Speed: 1 second up, 1 second down, no pauses.

1. Lying face-down on a high bench, hold light dumbbells in each hand

2. Lift the arms forward

3. Then out to the side

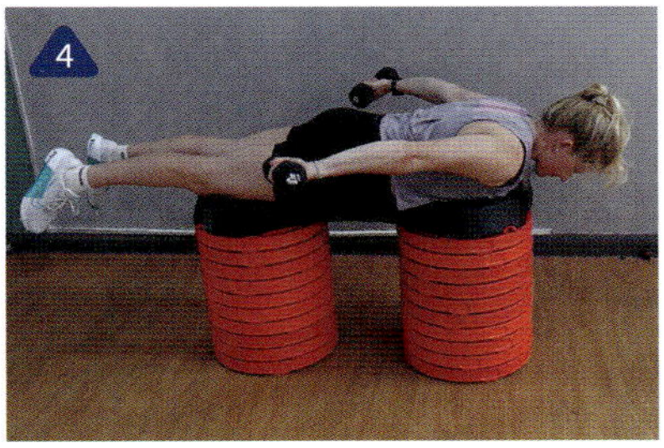

4. Then backward, before lowering again

Tip: Keep movements smooth and elbows soft. Imagine tracing slow, controlled arcs through the air rather than 'throwing' the weights up.

G.2. Curl & Press

Purpose: Combines arm and shoulder work for overall upper-body coordination and control – useful for trapeze adjustments and handling gear overhead.
Equipment: Dumbbells.
Recommended Training: 2 sets of 8-10 repetitions each arm. As usual, start light and use a load you could lift for 12-15 reps if needed. The final reps should feel controlled but challenging, not forced.
How To Do It: Stand tall with a dumbbell in each hand. Perform a bicep curl, then continue straight into a shoulder press. Lower in the same order. A natural turn of the wrist as the dumbbell moves overhead is fine. Alternate arms or lift together if preferred. Speed: 2 seconds up, no pause, 2 seconds down.

1. Stand tall with a dumbbell in each hand

2. Perform a bicep curl

3. Continue into a shoulder press, then lower in the same order

G.3. Military Press

(See p49)
Purpose: Builds shoulder and triceps strength for overhead strength.
Equipment: Dumbbells.
Recommended Training: 2 sets of 8-10 repetitions. Use a load you could lift for around 12 repetitions with good form. Prioritise control over weight, especially at the top of the press.
How To Do It: Stand with feet shoulder-width apart and knees slightly bent. Hold dumbbells or a barbell at shoulder height. Press upward until arms are nearly straight, then lower slowly. Keep the hands in line with your feet – not drifting forward – to stay balanced. Speed: 1 second up, no pause, 2 seconds down.

1. Stand with feet shoulder-width apart and knees slightly bent. Hold dumbbells or a barbell at shoulder height

2. Press upward until arms are nearly straight, then lower slowly

Tip: If your shoulders feel tight, try performing the movement seated or with lighter dumbbells.

G.4. Lateral Raises

Purpose: Strengthens the side (lateral) deltoids, helping maintain shoulder balance and improving sheet-handling posture.

Equipment: Dumbbells.

Recommended Training: 2 sets of 10-15 repetitions. Use very light dumbbells. As a guide, choose a load you could lift for 18-20 repetitions if needed. If you can't reach shoulder height with control, the weight is too heavy.

How To Do It: Stand with dumbbells at your sides and a slight bend in the elbows. Lift both arms out to the side until level with your shoulders, then lower slowly. Pretend you're a bird getting ready for take-off: if you can't reach horizontal, lighten the load before trying to fly. Speed: 1 second up, no pause, 1-2 seconds down.

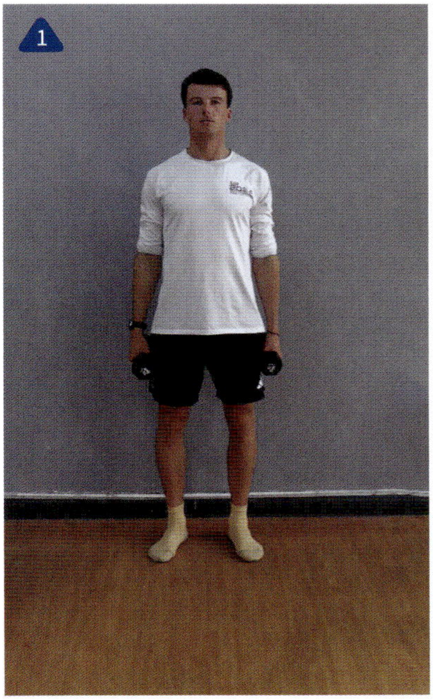

1. Stand with dumbbells at your sides and a slight bend in the elbows

2. Lift both arms out to the side until level with your shoulders, then lower slowly

H. Core Stability Exercises

Scan to watch video

These low-intensity exercises build the foundation for a strong, stable core. They help you control your core muscles and maintain spinal alignment – essential for balance, posture and hiking control.

You can include these in your routine three times a week, perhaps first thing in the morning or as a cooldown on training days. They don't take long, but the benefits accumulate.

H.1. Stretched-Out Stomach Suck

Purpose: Teaches you to activate the deep core muscles and flatten the lower back against the floor – the basis of all core control.

Equipment: None.

Recommended Training: 2 sets of 10 slow repetitions.

How To Do It: Lie flat on your back with legs extended and arms pointing to the ceiling. Draw your belly button down toward the floor to flatten the lower back. Slowly (over 2 seconds) lower your arms overhead until they just touch the floor, then return to vertical at the same pace. Keep the stomach tight throughout.

1. Lie flat on your back with legs extended and arms pointing to the ceiling. Draw your belly button down toward the floor to flatten the lower back

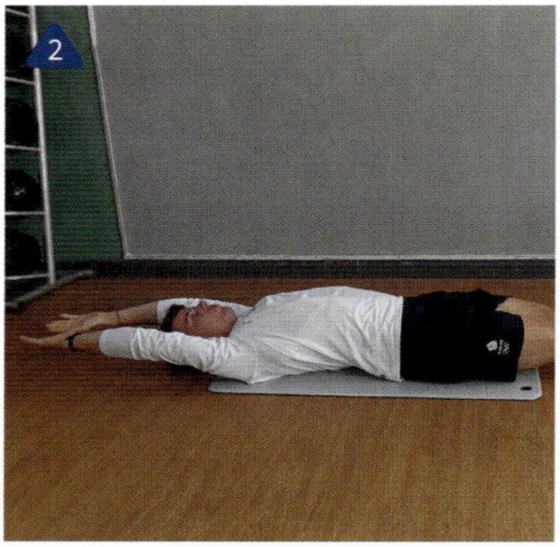

2. Slowly lower your arms overhead until they just touch the floor, then return to vertical

Tip: Move slowly and breathe normally – it's about control, not speed.

H.2. Side Leg Raises

Purpose: Strengthens the outer hip and trunk stabilisers that keep the pelvis level and help control side-to-side movement.

Equipment: None.

Recommended Training: 2 sets of 10-15 raises each side.

How To Do It: Lie on your side with upper leg straight. Lift the top leg 40-50cm, pause briefly, and lower slowly. Keep the body aligned with the top leg and the movement smooth. You can add a resistance band around the knees or ankles to increase the challenge.

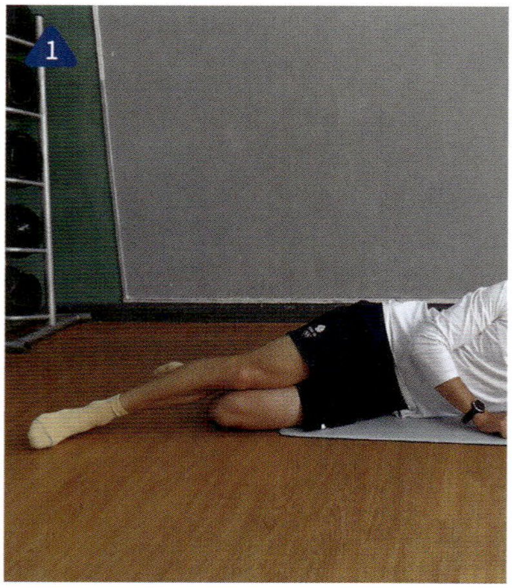

1. Lie on your side with legs straight and stacked

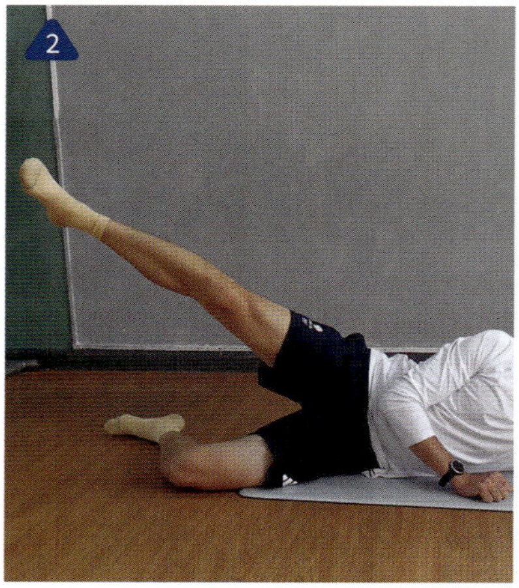

2. Lift the top leg to about 40-50cm, pause briefly, and lower slowly

H.3. Dead Bug

(See p39, 42, 47, 90)

Purpose: Trains anti-extension control of the trunk – teaching you to keep the spine stable while the limbs move, a fundamental part of hiking and trapezing.

Equipment: None.

Recommended Training: 2 sets of 8-12 slow repetitions each side.

1. Lie on your back with hips and knees at 90° and arms pointing to the ceiling. Flatten your lower back to the floor

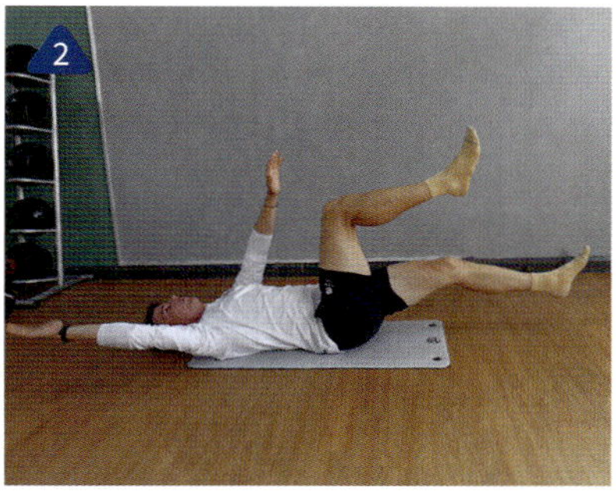

2. Slowly lower the opposite arm and leg until just above the ground, then return to the start and switch sides

How To Do It: Lie on your back with hips and knees bent to 90°, shins parallel to the floor and arms pointing straight up toward the ceiling. Gently press the lower back into the floor and maintain this contact throughout the exercise. Slowly lower one arm overhead while at the same time straightening the opposite leg and lowering it toward the floor (2 seconds). Stop just before either limb touches the ground, then return smoothly to the start position (2 seconds). Repeat on the other side.

The leg movement is a controlled straightening and lowering of the leg, not a drop to the floor. The pelvis and lower back should remain still throughout.

Variation:

Dead Bug with Weights: Add light dumbbells (1-4kg) to each hand for extra challenge.

Tip: If your lower back arches or lifts from the floor, shorten the range of motion or slow the movement further.

H.4. Controlled Single-Leg Half-Squat

Purpose: Improves single-leg stability and strengthens the glutes and trunk for balance when hiking or moving across the boat.

Equipment: None.

Recommended Training: 2 sets of 10 repetitions each leg.

How To Do It: Stand on one leg with the other bent behind you. Lower into a half-squat, allowing the knee to move over the big toe. Take two seconds down, hold one second at the bottom, and rise smoothly. Keep the hips level by tightening the glutes and core.

1. Stand on one leg with the other bent behind you

2. Lower into a half-squat, allowing the knee to move over the big toe

Tip: Imagine you're balancing on a small rock in the shallows – no wobbling allowed.

H.5. Copenhagen Plank

(See p33, 40, 41, 74, 90)

Purpose: Strengthens the adductors (inner thighs) and obliques – muscles important for hiking stability, balance on trapeze and injury prevention around the groin and hip.

Equipment: Low gym bench.

Recommended Training: 2 sets of 20-30-second holds each side.

How To Do It: Lie on your side beside a low padded gym bench. Support yourself on your forearm and place your top leg on the bench, lower leg hanging beneath it. Lift your hips so your body forms a straight line from head to foot. Hold while keeping the lower leg off the ground, then switch sides. Beginners can rest the lower knee on the floor for partial support.

Tip: Think about 'squeezing' the top leg into the bench – that inner-thigh effort is the point of the drill.

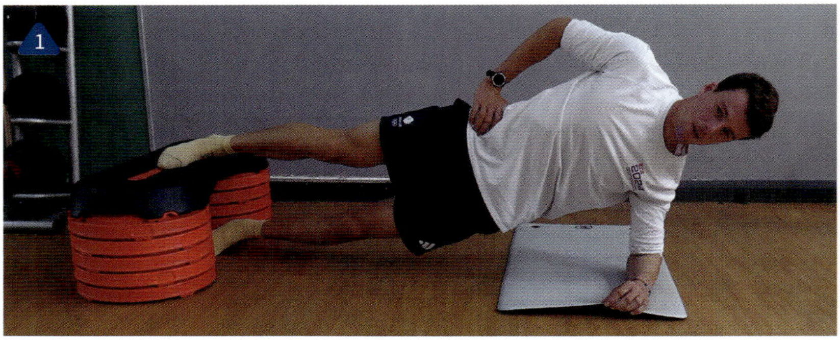

1. Lie on your side beside a bench. Support yourself on your forearm and place your top leg on the bench, lower leg hanging beneath it

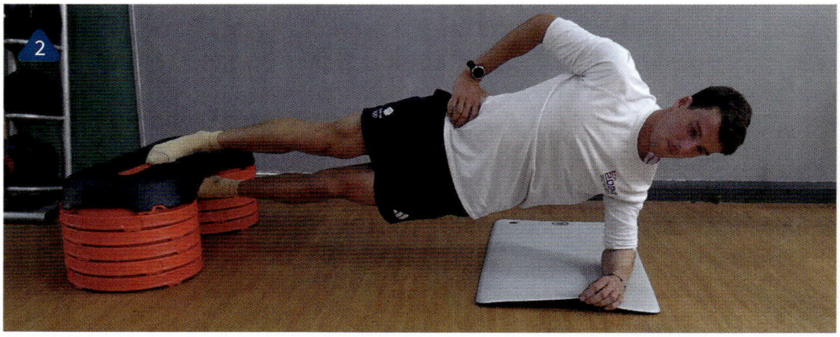

2. Lift your hips so your body forms a straight line from head to foot. Hold while keeping the lower leg off the ground

H.6. Bent Leg Raise

Purpose: Builds control of the lower core while teaching the spine to stay stable during leg movement – a key hiking skill.

Equipment: None.

Recommended Training: 2 sets of 10 repetitions each leg, holding each lift for about 10 seconds.

How To Do It: Lie on your back with knees bent and feet on the floor. Tighten your core, flatten the lower back, and lift one leg about 10cm. Hold, keeping the back flat, then lower and switch legs. Avoid excessive back arch and keep your core muscles working – draw your belly button towards the floor.

Tip: Keep the motion small and precise. If your lower back starts to lift, reset and try again – control is the goal.

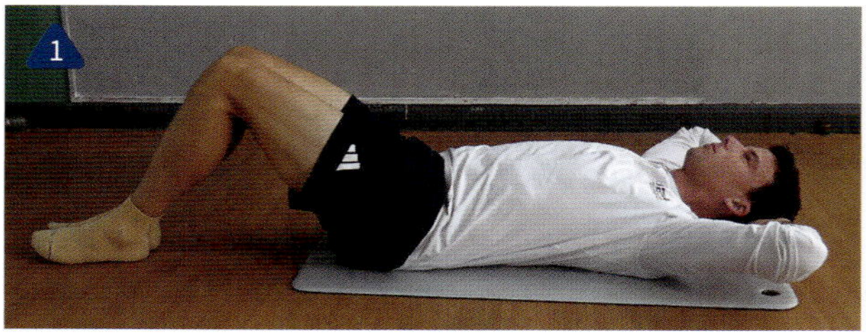

1. Lie on your back with knees bent and feet on the floor

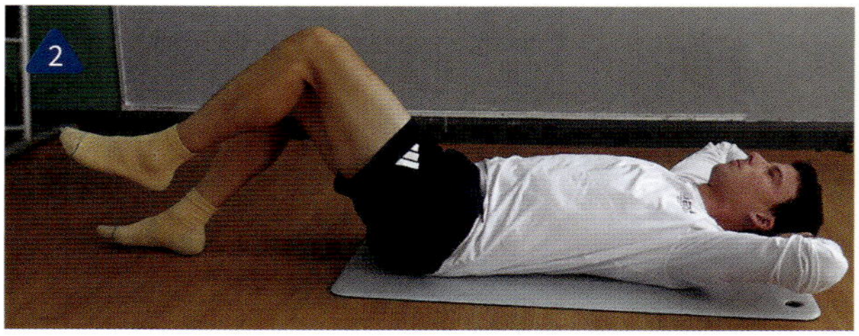

2. Tighten your core, flatten the lower back, and lift one leg about 10cm

H.7. Farmer's Carry (Suitcase Carry)

(See p39, 40, 41)

Purpose: Builds grip strength, trunk stability and resistance to side-bending – useful for hiking symmetry, carrying boats and general strength balance.

Equipment: Dumbbell(s) or kettlebell(s).

Recommended Training: 3 walks of 20-30m each side. As a guide, start with around 20-30% of body weight in one hand for the carry, or a load that makes the final 5-10m challenging to keep the torso upright without leaning.

1. Farmer's Carry with one hand

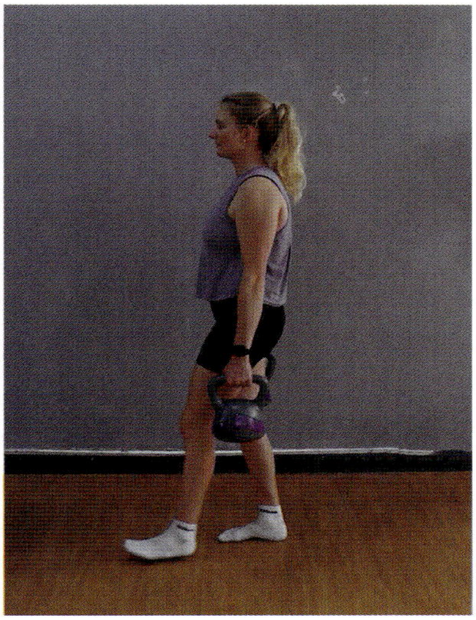

2. Farmer's Carry with two hands

How To Do It: Hold a heavy dumbbell or kettlebell in one hand by your side. Stand tall and walk slowly forward, keeping shoulders level and the torso upright. Turn around and switch hands on the way back. Alternatively, you can carry weights in both hands (classic Farmer's Carry) for more overall load (30-50% of body weight).

Tip: Imagine balancing a glass of water on your head – no leaning or wobbling.

Good Reading

Recommended books and articles relevant to sailing training.

Allen, J. & Jong, M. (2006). *Sailing and Sports Medicine: A Literature Review*. British Journal of Sports Medicine.

Blackburn, M.J. (1994). *Physiological responses to 90 minutes of simulated dinghy sailing*. Journal of Sports Sciences. 12:383-390.
The scientific report on my study on hiking.

Bompa, T. & Buzzichelli, C. (2015). *Periodization Training for Sports.*
A clear, practical guide to planning training over a season so athletes peak at the right time. While not sailing-specific, the ideas translate well to sailing, especially for building strength first and then converting it into sport-specific endurance.

Emmett, J. (2019). *Training to Win: Training exercises for solo boats, groups and those with a coach (Sail to Win).*
A very hands-on sailing book packed with on-water drills you can actually use, whether you're training alone, with a small group or alongside a coach. The focus is on smart, purposeful sessions that build boat handling, decision-making and race skills.

Gallwey, W.T. (1997). *The Inner Game of Tennis: The Classic Guide to the Mental Side of Peak Performance.*
'A tennis player first confronts the Inner Game when he discovers that there is an opponent inside his own head more formidable than the one across the net. He then realises that the greatest difficulty in returning a deep backhand lies not in the speed and placement of the ball itself, but in his mind's reaction to that ball: his own thinking makes the shot more difficult than it really is. Further, he becomes aware that these same mental obstacles which keep him from playing his best tennis also prevent him from living his best life.' Despite its focus on tennis, it is a great book that can help you improve your feel for and mental approach to sailing.

Lukins, J. (2019). *The Elite: Think Like an Athlete Succeed Like a Champion*
A concise playbook of elite athlete mindset habits for performing under pressure and winning consistently.

Orlick, T. (2007). *In Pursuit of Excellence.*
An easy read by a sports psychologist with great practical revelations and tips in areas like mental imagery, focusing, goal setting, working with coaches, self-confidence and control.

Spurway, N. (2006). *Hiking physiology and the 'quasi-isometric' concept*

Vogiatzis, I et al. (2011). *Quadriceps muscle blood flow and oxygen availability during repetitive bouts of isometric exercise in simulated sailing.* Journal of Sports Science

Winchombe, C. et al. (2025). *Coaches' insights: Determinants of athlete success, physical demands and training approaches in single-handed Olympic-class dinghy sailing.*

Acknowledgements

The author and publisher would like to thank those who have contributed to the development of this book.

We would like to thank:

- Micky Beckett, Matilda Nicholls, Jane Sunderland and Joe Rowe for demonstrating the exercises
- The management & staff of Everyone Active in Weymouth for welcoming us to use their gym for the photoshoot
- The athletes photographed as examples for our case studies: Amélie Renard (Ella), Edward Whittaker (Luke), Jess Powell (Sarah), William Whittaker (Doug), Peter Slater (Ian) and Diane Pepperdine (Margaret)

In terms of the photographs, all the photographs are either supplied by and copyright of Michael Blackburn or Fernhurst Books Limited, except those listed below.

Other photo credits / copyrights are:
Cover photo: Beau Outteridge / Australian Sailing Team
p18: Pixabay: Medienservice
p19 (bottom) Katy Barraclough
p22: Pixabay: kropekk_pl
p23: Sedat Yilmaz
p24: Tom Gruitt
p26: Michael Powell
p30: Zhik
p31 (left): Pro-Vela
p33: Pinnell & Bax
p39: Pexels: Jan van der Wolk
p43: Malcolm Lewin Photography
p55: LPB Aerial Imagery
p61: Alice Callow
p72: Pexels: Josué Rodríguez
p75, 79: William Whittaker
p76: Michael Powell
p77: Jane Sunderland
p81: Nigel Pepperdine
p84: Matilda Nicholls
p86: Paul Moreau
p91: Pixabay: AhmadArdity
p92: Pixabay: jplenio

We also appreciate the opportunity to extracts from two books published by Fernhurst Books:
p37: *Crewing To Win* by Saskia Clark (Olympic gold medallist)
p65: *Golden Lily – 10 Years On* by Lijia Xu (Olympic gold medallist)

TRAINING TO WIN
Jon Emmett
ANDREW SIMPSON FOUNDATION
THE SAILING CHARITY
Bart
29er
GBR 2493
GBR2381
sailingfast.co.uk
SAIL TO WIN

Take a look at some example pages from Training To Win by Jon Emmett

Practising 720s

A slight variation is practising 720s, but with the emphasis on keeping the speed up rather than making the circle as tight as possible.

Practising a 720° turn

Training Efficiently

As you move from the warm-up exercises to the core focus of the training session, you need to ensure that you keep working efficiently. Just sitting around waiting, with sails flapping, can risk undoing all the benefits of training. In addition to potentially damaging equipment in strong winds, it wastes the sailors' concentration and can lead to them getting too hot or too cold in extreme conditions. When cold they need to keep moving; when very hot we need to limit their time on the water. In short, it does no one any good! Sessions should be all about quality not quantity.

Follow-My-Leader

If you are going into a specific exercise and the group is spread over an area, Follow-My-Leader is a great way of rounding up the group. Here the sailors must match the speed and direction of the boat in front and the RIB can use it to gather up the group. We will be dealing with this more in later chapters.

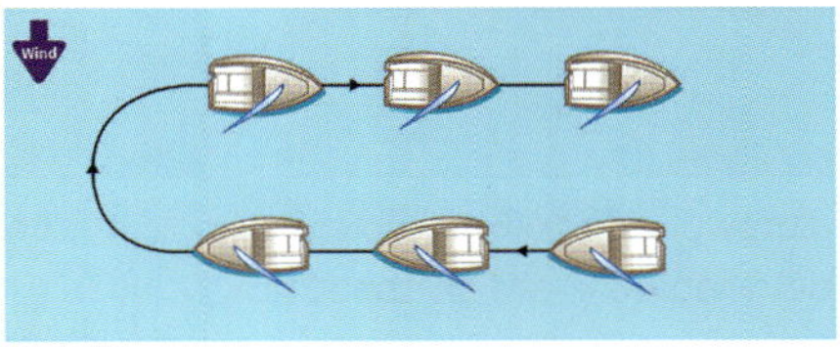

Follow-My-Leader

For Follow-My-Leader, boats must be:

- Equally spaced (the stronger the wind the greater the distance needed between the boats)
- Sailing at equal speed (try both completely stopped and full speed!)
- An equal distance upwind (otherwise one or more boats would get an advantage)

Again, people can join in Follow-My-Leader as soon as they arrive.

Gybing Upwind & Tacking Downwind

The first is that you change the upwind exercise so that you have to gybe rather than tack. Let me repeat that: when going upwind you have to gybe (no tacks allowed). You could also have it that you have to tack going downwind as well!

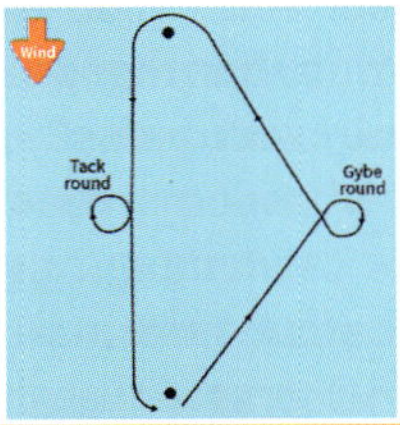

Triple Gybes & Triple Tacks

The other option is a triple gybe (when you want to gybe) and you could have to triple tack when going upwind.

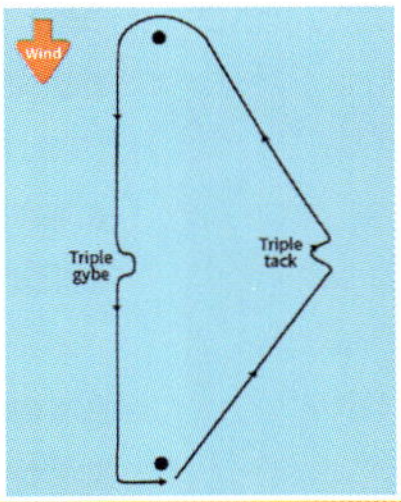

Different Tacks Downwind

In this exercise two boats start on opposite gybes downwind and gybe on the whistle. This is to see which, if any, gybe provides better VMG to the downwind mark and, particularly for single-handers, allow them to practise sailing on port gybe.

The feel of this is very different to racing when sailors usually get to choose when they will gybe, change angle etc. For example, sailors sailing with unstayed rigs may be very used to sailing downwind mainly on starboard tack because, from a rules point of view, you are safer. However, port tack may be faster because of the angle to waves or the ability to get to the wind you want etc. Sometimes it is hard to put a finger on the reason, but one tack is just faster!

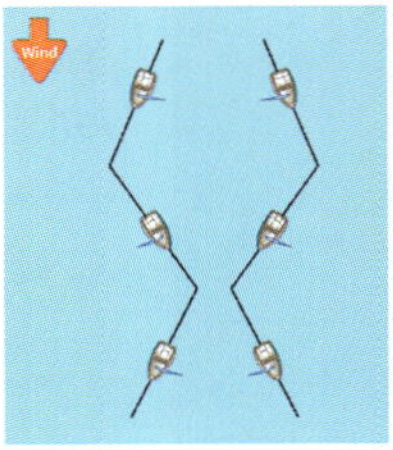

Progression

Increasing the difficulty is very important when it comes to boat-handling training: the more difficult the exercise, the easier it will make winning on the race course. You must always push your comfort levels; confidence as well as competence is very important. For example, if you train in 30 knots, suddenly racing in 25 knots seems much easier.

So, with the alternate mark roundings, we can look at altering the rounding every lap (after the first). Here are 3 examples:

1. Different Rounding Windward & Leeward:

	Windward mark rounding	Leeward mark rounding
Lap 1	Port	Port
Lap 2	Starboard	Port
Lap 3	Port	Starboard
Repeat even laps	Starboard	Port
Repeat odd laps	Port	Starboard

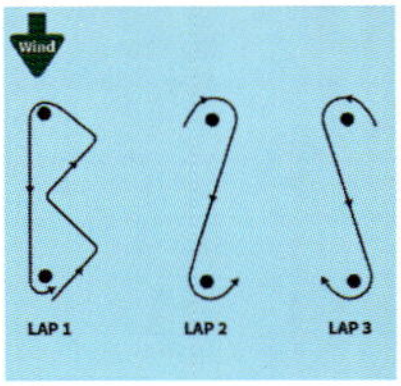

2. Same Windward (can be done either port or starboard, this time shown as port) **But Leeward Mark Changes:**

	Windward mark rounding	Leeward mark rounding
Lap 1	Port	Port
Lap 2	Port	Starboard
Lap 3	Port	Port
Repeat even laps	Port	Starboard
Repeat odd laps	Port	Port

3. Or the more complex, Change One Mark At A Time:

	Windward mark rounding	Leeward mark rounding
Lap 1	Port	Port
Lap 2	Starboard	Port
Lap 3	Starboard	Starboard
Repeat even laps	Port	Starboard
Repeat odd laps	Port	Port

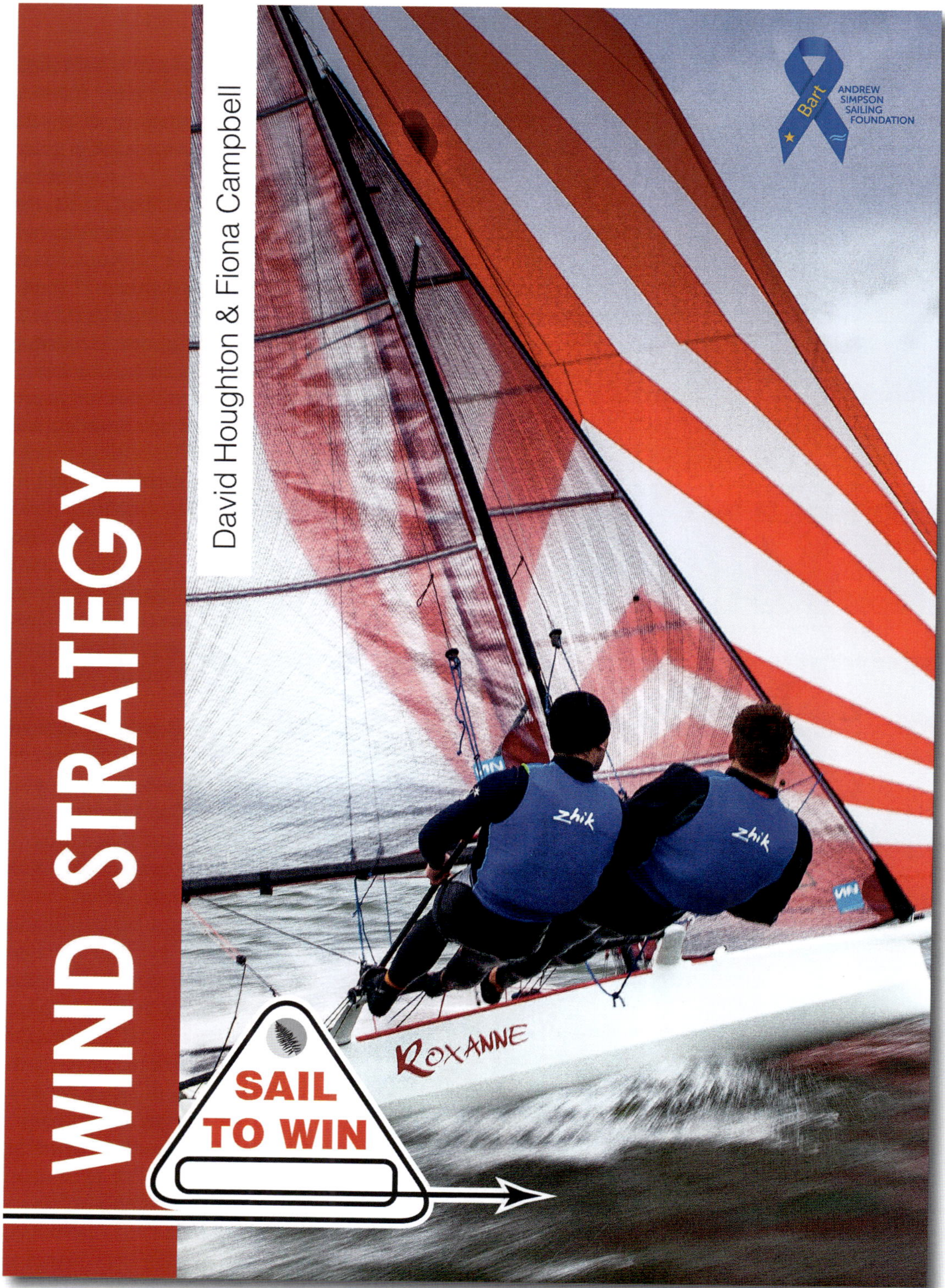
WIND STRATEGY
David Houghton & Fiona Campbell
Bart
ANDREW SIMPSON SAILING FOUNDATION
SAIL TO WIN
zhik
zhik
ROXANNE

Take a look at some example pages from Wind Strategy by David Houghton & Fiona Campbell

CHAPTER 2
The Sailor's Wind

Anything moving requires energy to start it off, and in most cases to keep it going. The wind is no exception. Air moves around the Earth in response to heating by the sun. Equatorial regions receive the most heat, polar regions the least. The major wind systems of the world are all the result of heated air rising over equatorial regions and being replaced by colder air from polar regions. The zone where the major cold and warm winds meet is commonly known as the polar front, and is the birthplace of many of the larger weather systems – the depressions and anticyclones – of temperate latitudes.

The traditional (and easiest) way to map the movements of air around the world is to plot the values of pressure, or weight of air, at the Earth's surface. Such weather maps with their lines of equal pressure – isobars – have been in use for over a hundred years, ever since the invention of the electric telegraph. Weather satellites have provided pictorial evidence of the size, shape and main characteristics of depressions and anticyclones, the clouds acting as dye in the air to map out their development and decay.

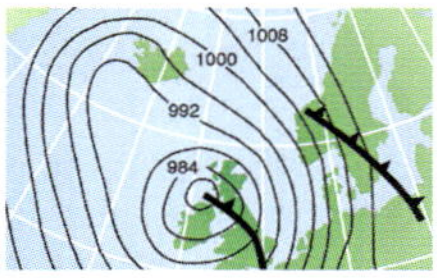

A snippet of a weather map

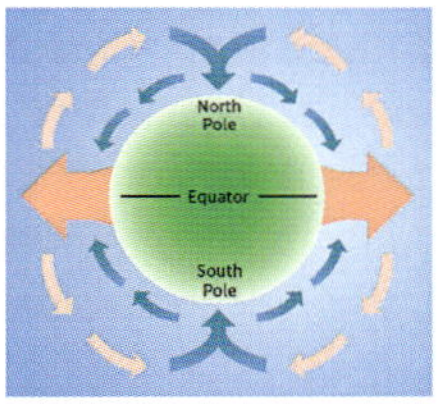

In its simplest form: Heated air rises over the equator to be replaced by cooler air from the poles

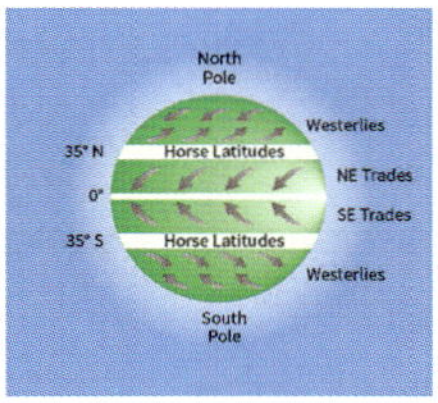

Due to land and the Earth's rotation, this simple cell model (left) is modified (above)

13

CHAPTER 3 Wind Facts: Coasts, Lakes & Islands

Wind Blowing Along The Shore

With a wind blowing parallel or nearly parallel to the coast there is a major difference in wind within about 10 kilometres of the shore depending on whether the land is on your right or left hand side when facing into the wind. You will see below that, with the land on your left looking upwind, the different angles of the surface winds over land and sea are convergent for the same pressure gradient wind, resulting in a band of stronger wind near the shore. The increase in wind speed in the band is in the order of 25%, e.g. 5 knots added to a 20-knot wind. The converging airstreams often give more cloud near the coast, sometimes enough to produce a shower or two.

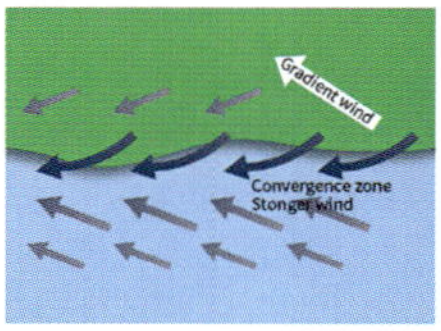

Coastal convergence

There is no precise figure for the distance from the shore of the strongest wind. On a straight coast it is generally between 2 and 5 kilometres off. On an irregular coast the wind will blow so as to smooth out the irreglarities, sometimes strongest close inshore, sometimes strongest further out. In the case of headlands separated by a shallow bay, the band of strong wind will extend from headland to headland, being close inshore at each headland.

The stronger wind just offshore is sometimes mistaken for a sea breeze. A race in the English Channel saw some boats headed out to sea off Brighton as dusk approached, assuming that the wind inshore would die away, only to find that those that stayed 2 to 3 kilometres off benefited from an extra few knots of easterly wind all night.

If you are racing in a wind aligned in this way to the coast you can be reasonably sure not only of finding a strong wind band but also that it will remain in the same place throughout the race. Do not overlook the possible benefit of using the more backed, though lighter, wind close to the shore where it will be coming off the land. When racing in the West Solent, for instance, in a south-westerly it is sometimes preferable to make Yarmouth Buoy on a single tack close inshore (below) rather than opting for a favourable tide a kilometre further off and a series of short tacks in a more veered wind.

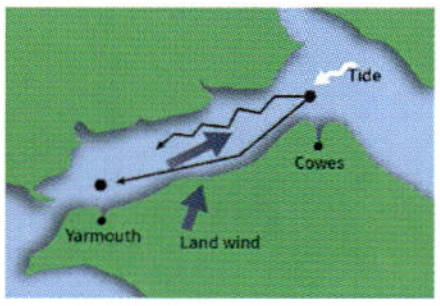

Racing in the West Solent

In the opposite case, of the land on your right looking upwind, the two airstreams diverge (below) and the wind is generally lighter within a few kilometres of the shore. Because of this divergence the air tends to subside near the coast, and this clears, or at least thins, any low cloud which might be around. This is why the

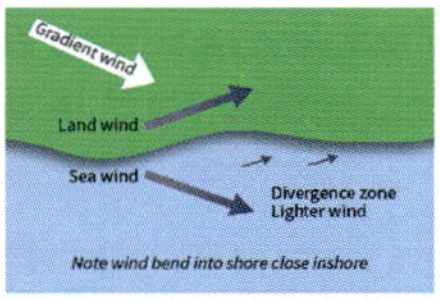

Coastal divergence

21

CHAPTER 6
Wind Facts:
Southern Hemisphere

All the features of the wind described in Chapters 2, 3, 4 and 5 are experienced in the Southern Hemisphere. The arguments are virtually identical but, because the influence of the earth's rotation is reversed, the wind bends in the opposite direction relative to the pressure gradient. Many of the relevant diagrams therefore are mirror images of those for the Northern Hemisphere. The following is a summary of the facts about the wind in the same sequence as has been followed in Chapters 2 to 5.

Pressure Gradient & Surface Winds, Stability & Friction

There is a pressure gradient wind, which can be measured from the isobars using the Geostrophic Scale on p14. Buys Ballot's Law for the Southern Hemisphere states that, if you stand with your back to the wind, low pressure will be to your right-hand side (below).

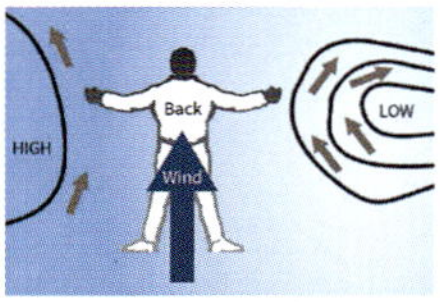

Buys Ballot's Law in Southern Hemisphere

Because of friction the surface wind is slowed, but its direction is veered compared to the wind aloft, more so over land than over water (right). The temperature of the land and sea relative to the air determines the buoyancy of the air and the ability of the wind aloft to get down to the surface.

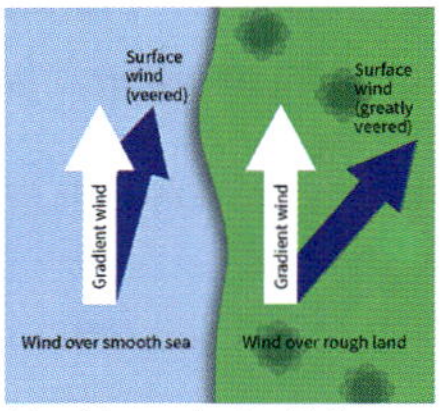

Surface wind over smooth sea & rough land

There is a diurnal variation in wind between day and night.

The other illustrations within Chapter 2 are the same for both Hemispheres. Gusts and lulls occur, and when the gusts are the result of the air aloft coming down to the surface the gust backs.

30

WIND STRATEGY

Quadrant 1

This defines the range of gradient wind directions for the best sea breezes; between west and north on a south-facing coast, between south and west on an east-facing coast, and so on. Sea breezes may reach as much as 20 to 25 knots when the pressure gradient wind is in this quadrant. Many a sailor has been caught out assuming a dying offshore breeze mid-morning meant light winds for the rest of the day, when in fact it indicated ideal conditions for the best possible sea breeze.

The normal sequence of events starts with an early morning wind blowing offshore; then towards mid-morning, as the land warms, this breeze dies close to the shore and an onshore breeze begins, usually before midday. It is very shallow at first; smoke from tall chimneys still going straight upwards or even offshore. Over the next 2 to 3 hours the new sea breeze builds steadily, simultaneously pushing inland and extending seawards. It also veers, quickly at first, and then more slowly until it settles down blowing from a direction about 20 degrees back from the general line of the coast (below). The calm which precedes the new breeze – a zone of virtually no wind about 100 to 300 metres wide – moves out seawards ahead of it. The developing sea breeze is strongest inshore at every stage, and lightest at its seaward extremity.

If the initial surface wind direction is nearly parallel to the coast (bottom) – and so long as there is a component of the gradient wind offshore – the onset of the sea breeze will merely back the wind near the shore, rather than kill it altogether. This backed wind extends seawards, increasing and veering to the final sea breeze direction, 20 degrees off the shoreline.

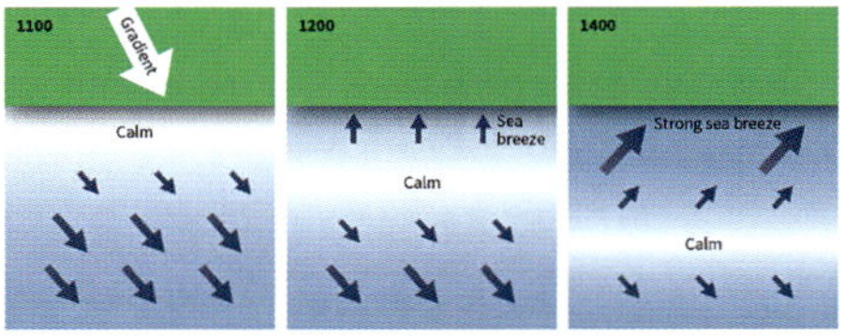

Typical stages in the development of a sea breeze with a Quadrant 1 gradient wind. Coast may face in any direction

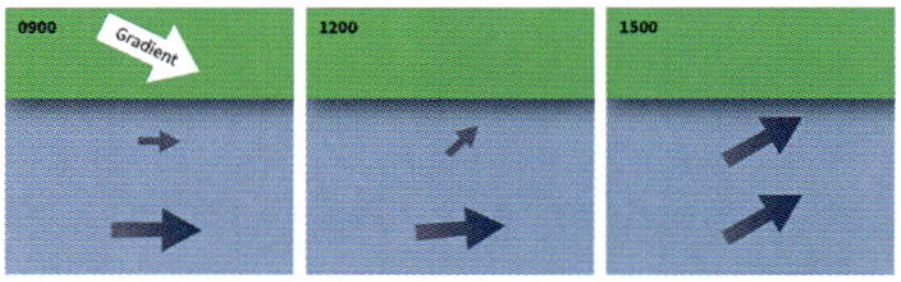

Typical stages in the development of a sea breeze with the surface wind nearly parallel to the coast

42

SAIL
TO WIN
Taking a fresh look at the complex subject of racing to get you moving up the leaderboard
FITNESS TO WIN
COACH YOURSELF TO WIN
HELMING TO WIN
TACTICS TO WIN
TUNING TO WIN
TRAINING TO WIN
CREWING TO WIN
WIND STRATEGY
OPTIMIST RACING
TACTICS MADE SIMPLE
LASER CAMPAIGN MANUAL
MASTERING DATA TO WIN
View our entire list at **www.fernhurstbooks.com**
Sign up to receive details of new books & exclusive special offers at **www.fernhurstbooks.com/register**
Get to know us more on **social media**
FERNHURST BOOKS